Agile Project Management

The Complete Guide for Beginners to Scrum,

Agile Project Management, and Software

Development

Table of Contents

Introduction

There are a lot of questions that revolve around the fields of project and software development. Is this programming language better than the others? Should we allow others to do the testing or should we do it ourselves? What bugs must one deal with in every phase of the development process? And so on and so forth.

But the most pressing question that managers often have to deal with is this: Can things be done at a faster and more effective pace? As someone who has been managing projects for years now, I could tell that you that is not technical and inherent problems that anyone involved in a project gets the most worked up about.

Coding issues? Let someone who knows the language deal with it? Bugs and glitches? A tester can find and identify them through their work? The software engine not compatible with the program? Perhaps replacing it with one that does will do the trick.

It is on the things that revolve outside of the work of teams that give managers the most problems. The constant need to coordinate teams, the dealing with deadlines, inter-team communication issues, and the logistics of human resources and technical skills. These are the things that keep everyone involved in a project awake at night; metaphorically and literally speaking.

And if that was not enough, you would have to deal with pressure from the higher-ups who may or may not know how the development process goes but insists on having things done in one way. Worse is if they insist on seeing results within a ludicrously short period of time or, without a notice, change goals and deadlines which your team has to adapt to ASAP.

More often than not, it is in finding a balance between being speedy and producing the desired results where managers often find the most pressing of challenges at during the project development process. Without a doubt, having to make sure everybody is one the same page in meeting goals while also making sure that the end product kind of works is a rather difficult task for most managers and leads.

But what if I were to tell you that there is a way to make things faster and more convenient? And not only does it make things easier for you, it allows you to produce the desired results in time or earlier. This is where Agile Project Management comes into play and might save you and your team from a lot of pressure, stress, and frustration in the development process.

What is the Agile Project Management methodology, exactly?

Without giving away too much (since you'll be reading about it for the entire book), the agile methodology is merely adopting a management style that is adaptive to whatever happens in the middle of a project without losing sight of the need to finish whatever was started in the soonest time possible.

What you have to understand is that a project is like clockwork. If you want things to run as smoothly as possible, you must make sure that everything not only functions but that said functions ultimately contribute to the attainment of a goal.

It's easy to bring in the best resources for a project, it's an entirely different thing to make sure everything is in sync and working towards a common goal. And not only should everything be working together but should remain so as you and your team have to address any changes and adjustments made to the plan.

Of course, you will learn how Agile came to be and why it would be an ideal strategy to implement in your project. And when you learn why it works, you should be able to identify the different strategies that you can use to make the methodology compatible with your group's current layout.

As with a lot of management methodologies, Agile is not a one-trick pony. As a matter of fact, it is so lenient that it allows you to implement the method through 4 different frameworks: Scrum, X, Kanban, and Lean. In this book, you will learn how each principle can be implemented, what makes them different from one another, and which is best according to your current project.

However, talking about implementing these changes would not be enough if your team itself is not willing to embrace the changes. As such, you would also learn how your team handles changes in the middle of the development process and what you can do to make the transition more comfortable for them.

You would also learn what motivates entire teams to complete common goals and, alternatively, what hinders them from reaching the same or impede others from contributing to it. It is by understanding how a team thinks as a group and individually would you be able to help them become more effective in implementing the methodologies that you are about to learn.

Such implementations, in turn, allowed the project leads to yield tremendous results from their projects. By learning how these methodologies have been implemented in the past, you may be able to identify how you can implement the same in your project or build on their successes by doing something even better.

But of course, we'd have to address the elephant in the room: can this methodology work for your project? The answer is always a yes. The beauty with Agile is that, for all its seemingly technical nature, is actually a rather simple process to follow.

The methodology helps you by breaking down the more complex aspects of your project and make your team focus on the most pressing of tasks and problems. This way, you and your team can deliver value to clients and eliminate a lot of waste on your development processes on a regular basis.

Just do remember that the success Agile Project Management methodology is reliant on how well you implement it on your project. As such, it is best that you learn as much of it in the simplest and most straightforward of terms possible. And this is where this book would into play.

If you have no further questions, let us head on and master the art of implementing the Agile Project Management methodology.

Chapter I: The Basics of Agile Project Management

What is Agile Project Management, Exactly?

This might be the first question that will pop up in your head and it is best that we answer it first. The most basic definition of APM is that is a methodology in which work is completed and delivered in short cycles (sometimes called sprints) and tweaked over time. This is done with the goal of providing value through increasing performance results as well as improving the structure of the project plan. This has similar features as most project planning and management methods in which the entire project is divided into smaller tasks.

The goal of the methodology is to simply cut out the cost by doing away with the trial-and-error strategy used by many project managers. By using a more cautious and yet proactive approach to project, one should be able to get better results from it.

Sounds straightforward, right? If you are still wondering what the style is, it would be better if we compare it to other methodologies.

The Flaws of the Classic Method

The classic project management method is simply the methodology that every manager typically uses as a default. It can differ from one manager to another but it mostly manifests the same flaws in each project. They are the following:

A. Too Much Time on the Planning Phase

A major flaw with the classic project management method is that you are planning the entire project up front. This means that you would spend more time finding the resources, evaluating costs, and assigning tasks and schedules for your team to follow.

The problem here is that a major portion of the time you spent for planning your strategy can be used more productively like actually executing the plans. And the long time spent on planning also leaves the method open for another flaw which is...

B. Plans Become Inflexible Eventually

When you spend too much time on planning, you become dead-set on implementing it no matter what. A lot of managers do this because they don't want to waste all that mental energy they have spent creating the plan.

However, this does mean that the plan does not account for changes in the middle of the process. There will always be a chance that new deadlines have to be met which, in turn, requires for the acquisition of new resources, the reshuffling of teams, and evaluation of new costs. This means that you can easily shoot over the budget and make the development process even more chaotic than necessary.

C. Treating the Team as Mere Resources

During planning, miscalculations can occur. Tasks or even entire projects could get underestimated. This would usually result in changes in schedule and resource allocations.

If you are not careful in this phase, you are inadvertently giving the impression that your team is expendable. Worse, you could just attribute failure in implementation of the changes over the team. This can increase animosity between teams and team members which ultimately impedes everybody from achieving shared goals.

What Makes Agile Project Management Different

More often than not, it is preferred that you use any other methodology instead of the standard method. This is where Agile Project Management comes into play and it has a few characteristics that instantly set it apart from the standard method.

1. **It is Segmented by Design**

The agile methodology is comprised of several "iterations" that last about 4 weeks. This can help managers in the sense that it makes evaluation all the easier to perform on a regular basis.

Also, the subdividing of the larger project into several iterations can psychologically help managers and team members focus on develop specific parts of the project. If one part of the project has to be done in a later iteration, then there is no need to worry about completing its sub-goals; just yet.

2. **It is Based on Time Periods**

In as much as projects in the agile method are divided into segments, each segment itself has a fixed time period. As was stated, each iteration can last up to a month and this cannot be modified down the line if the team agrees to such conditions.

With their efforts focused on one part of the project for a short period of time, the agile method can help teams become more productive and generate observable results within each iteration. And this is even if there are changes brought about by outside forces during each cycle.

3. It is Easy to Understand, even for Non-Tech Folk

One of the problem areas in project management is actually in communicating progress to clients, shareholders, and other people who might not have a good grasp on the more technical aspects of your work. In some methodologies, progress is either rarely communicated on a regular basis as they are long-term in nature. Basically, there is nothing to report regularly as overall goals take a while to be achieved.

And if some goals are short term, they are communicated in a manner that is highly technical and confusing. All the clients see are pretty graphs and numbers. Nothing about it seems to inspire their minds or give them the assurance that everything is running according to the plan.

Since the agile method runs on iterations, clients and the powers-that-be in your company can be certain of regular reports regarding the progress of a project. And not only will the reports be regular, they are presented in a manner that is easy to understand. This should give the clients an impression of what is going on and what to expect next.

The Principles of the Agile Method

So, what makes the Agile methodology work? The truth is that the method is guided by 12 principles that help managers implement the method properly and get the results they expected from the project or more.

And the best part about these principles? They are actually quite easy to remember. They are as follows:

1. **"Our highest priority is to satisfy the customer through early and continuous delivery of valuable software (or whatever else you deliver)".**

In the agile method, the focus is always on providing clients with updates on the progress of software. With this method, it is so easy for anyone to see that there have been progresses made in the project and that such progresses are observable. Through regular reports at the end of each iteration, a client can get an idea as to how a project is ultimately going to look and feel like once it is completed.

The method also takes into consideration any input that the client gives. After all, the software should be the ultimate expression of what the client has envisioned. Anything less than that is never acceptable.

2. "Welcome changing requirements, even late in development. Agile processes harness change for the customer's competitive advantage."

Unlike other methods which balk at the idea of constant changes, the agile method embraces it to the fullest. For the agile method, change is but a mere opportunity that can enhance the project and help the team complete it in the soonest time possible.

This is something noteworthy as changes can occur even in the later stages of the development process. And such changes can be frustrating as they can drastically change the buildup of the end product. With the agile method, you can anticipate for such changes and build the software in a manner that makes it compatible to the same if they were to pop up in each iteration.

3. "Deliver projects frequently, from a couple of weeks to a couple of months, with a preference for the shorter timescale."

This might sound contradictory to what has been said but it is vital to the success of the agile method that you stick to the development cycles. Even if you finish early and have a working product to present to the client, don't rush things through but instead, allow for reworks and testing until the cycle is complete.

Changes might happen in the middle of the process but a manager must be able to keep their team focused on what needs to be done and produce results within each time period. This way, progress can be seen either in small steps or big leaps forward.

4. "Coordinating team members must work together daily throughout the project."

The stakeholders of the company must also know of whatever is happening in the project. As such, your team and the higher-ups must have an open and transparent line of communication so that concerns at both sides are aired out and addressed efficiently.

On the manager's part, they should know exactly when shareholders and upper management would like some changes made in the project. This way, they can communicate the same to their team as quickly as possible and adjust the work accordingly.

5. **"Build projects around motivated individuals. Give them the environment and support they need and trust them to get the job done."**

All the best equipment and a good team setup would not matter if your team is not made up of highly motivated people. In fact, the agile method is highly dependent on the ability of people to maintain a motivated mindset when at work.

This can be a rather tall order since change, by nature, can be discouraging. Some of your team members might even feel frustrated by the lack of consistency when it comes to the overall plan.

This is where you as a manager would play a crucial role in as you can rally your troops to do what they do best but also diplomatically tell them to make some course corrections. The more efficient you are in helping your team stay motivate but accepting of changes, the faster you can finish your projects and in good quality to boot.

6. **"Face-to-face conversation is the most efficient and effective method of conveying information to and within different teams."**

The stream of information within your team and outside should not only remain open. It should also be simple. The line of communication in agile project management must be so straight that there is only one source, one messenger at a time, and receivers at every team and level.

With this, you can make sure that information you receive from the higher-ups and clients are the most accurate so you can quickly relay the same to your team. This also works in reverse if your team wants to inform outside people of what is going in the project.

In practice, they should relay the information to their leader who is going to relay it to you and you will then report the same to your superiors. The simpler the line of communication is, fewer chances there will be of crucial information being lost in translation and never acted on.

7. "The final product is the primary measure of progress."

How could you tell if your team is making progress under the method? The answer is if the end product for each iteration works. This is why you should push your team to produce something functional at the end of each iteration for the clients and shareholders to test for themselves.

However, you have to be careful that you do not rush things through. It is often a mistake that managers make to overwork their team just to produce something decent to present in the next report. If possible, just give them a compelling reminder to get things done and tested before the iteration ends.

Also, make sure that the product gradually changes in each iteration. If it was functional in the first, then make sure it is enhanced in the next. Do this until the product is in its best possible version upon the completion of all iterations.

8. "Agile processes promote sustainable development. All stakeholders should be able to maintain a constant pace indefinitely."

The workflow of your project should not be mired by periods of inactivity. Every iteration should focus on one aspect of the project so that milestones could be met at the end of every cycle.

The momentum of your team in every project must be so strong that you do not stop building on what has been achieved so far. In other methods, there are periods during which things stop as people wait for the necessary resources. To avoid this, set up milestones and deadlines for your team that are easy to meet but produce observable results.

9. "Continuous attention to technical excellence and good design enhances agility."

This might be basic but the software you are producing should be designed with functionality in mind. Combine this with the agile project management method and your team should be able to produce something functional at the end of each cycle.

However, you must also build on the functionality. If it works in the first time, then it must work in the next instance that you would present the same product to clients and shareholders. This constant improvement on the functionality and design of the product should give the impression to outside elements that your team is working on something that is eventually going to be great upon release.

10. "Simplicity—the art of maximizing the amount of work not done—is essential."

The core essence of the Agile Project Management method is that you don't waste time. And there is nothing more time-wasting than needless elaboration. Make sure that you get the basics of the product's design first before you complicate things with new features and functionalities.

Aside from the product, this also applies to the culture of the team as well. Every task that you assign to them must be met with the corresponding amount of effort depending on the urgency of the task. In essence, do not make the team work harder if not necessary but make sure that they greet every new task with the same amount of zeal and drive.

11. "The best architectures, requirements, and designs emerge from self-organizing teams."

In the agile method, constant supervision or (as I would like to call it) excessive hand-holding is never recommended. Your team must possess the initiative to get things done at the right time without you having to tell them constantly how to do their jobs.

The reason for this is that in-company politics and bureaucracy can get in the way of finishing things on time. If your team can solve problems without raising an alarm to the higher-ups, just let them be so that they can get the project done in the soonest time possible.

12. "At regular intervals, the team reflects on how to become more effective, then tunes and adjusts its behavior accordingly."

One element of the agile method is the ability to adapt to new conditions. This means that a team must regularly consider how they can improve on their work. As such, you as the manager must conduct regular meetings to discuss the team's performance in every iteration.

Where did the team excel at? Where was it lacking? Such things can be answered by looking at the end result for each cycle. Once problems are identified, all that is left to do is to address such and do better in the next cycle.

These principles are best if everybody knows about them and, to an extent, is constantly reminded about them. Post these principles in the workplace as much as you can so people can get the reminder that they need and produce the best possible results out of their work.

How is the Agile Method Done?

The Agile Project Method, regardless of what principle you will use, is always focused on dividing the entire workload into smaller sections. By doing this, a manager instantly makes their project more attainable with set milestones in each section.

In essence, a manager makes the project easier to complete by giving each section its defined set of supplementary goals and objects. With this, it is easier to identify what needs to be developed further or what must be looked back at a later phase of the development process.

After each cycle, the team will then have a meeting with you, the upper management, the shareholders, and the clients. There, progresses will be presented and the product given a demonstration (if possible). An exchange of ideas is also possible as stakeholders can critique the progress and the team can air out concerns that the upper management can address.

The biggest benefit with the agile method is that any problem that arises is addressed and corrected before things get out of hand. It also makes sure that everybody is on the same page and communications remain as transparent as possible.

Project Roles

Teams under the agile method, regardless of their chosen strategy, should always work like gears on a machine. Everyone should know the role they play in the project and what they can contribute to its success.

As such, it is important that managers outline each key role that team members and outside persons can play in the development process. Regardless of how you name the roles for your team, they should at least follow the sequence like the one below.

A. The Product Owner

This is the person who is in charge with communicating information between the clients, the stakeholders, and the team developing the product. To be a product owner, a person must be knowledgeable of the product as well as the vision and needs of the clients.

Also, they are required to work with the development team on a daily basis so that they are on track with the time period for each iteration. If it is not a dead giveaway already, this role will be assigned to managers or, to put it more bluntly, you.

B. The Development Team

This is the group assigned for creating the product from the ground up. Since the development process is a long and arduous one that takes up multiple phases and requires different sub-processes, it is advisable that you divide the team even further into sub groups.

For instance, one team can serve as the main designing group, the others will work on the programming, the others will work as bug and glitch fixers, and the others can fulfill other supplementary roles such as designers, code engineers, and testers.

Regardless of how you divide the teams, it is necessary that you make sure that everyone is hands-on in the project. This prevents anyone from excusing themselves if things don't go as planned or, alternatively, make sure everyone is able to celebrate on every success achieved.

C. The Scrum Master

Also known as the Project Facilitator, the Scrum Master plays a huge role in supporting the development team. In essence, they serve as a liaison between the team and the company's administration, eliminating potential roadblocks in the communication system so that information and other resources flow freely in between groups.

To be a Scrum master, one must have a strong understanding of the concept of servant leadership. They are the ones that work closely with the development team and will report to outside groups as to what the team has achieved so far.

D. Stakeholders and Upper Management

Although not directly involved in the development process, these individuals can still provide valuable input for the team to consider. They might have a perspective on the product that the team did not look into but would ultimately help in improving it.

As such, the goal in working with these people is to maintain a communication that is honest, transparent, and open. Development teams should not feel intimidated by the higher-ups in relaying their concerns and the higher-ups, in turn, would not feel left out of the development process.

This is why regular meetings are necessary in making sure everyone within the team and outside knows what the other is doing. This also helps in addressing issues between groups which should help in speeding up the development process.

E. The Mentor

The Mentor is simply someone who already has an experience in implementing the agile method in previous projects. It is their role to provide tips when needed and guide everybody else through the implementation phase.

Although mentors are not directly involved in the development of the software, they are still invaluable as their tips in applying the principles would ultimately affect the quality of the end product. Due to nature of the Mentor's role, you can have someone from outside the team and even outside the company fill in this position. A consultant is most recommended for the role although there is no stopping you from seeking advice from other executives and managers.

Inherent Flaws

With all of these said and done, is the Agile Project Management method a perfect strategy? Sadly, the answer is No. It is not for every project or for every management style out there as it possesses two inherent flaws.

1. It is Easy to Lose Track

By breaking down a project into several smaller sections, you actually run the risk of losing sight of the overall goal. Instead of one goal that everybody must do their best in order to meet, you have now multiple vital goals that must be met but may not automatically contribute to the larger goal.

As such, due to this flaw, it is rather important that you get everyone involved during meetings. Stakeholders should be able to present their vision, upper management provide the guidance, and the development teams given the chance to air out their concerns.

The point here is that everyone should be able to provide a perspective to the project that is focused on meeting the larger goals. If at least one person knows that the project can stray off the path or has strayed off, then the chances of a major course correction later on may be minimized.

This is why it is also necessary that you make it a habit to regularly call for meetings. Perhaps everyone can get so engrossed in their short-term goals that they forget that they are supposed to align their work to ultimately contribute to the larger project goals. Through regular meetings, everyone can get in touch with everybody and make sure everyone is working to meet common goals.

2. **It is Heavily Dependent on Quick Decision Making**

Due to the adaptive nature of the method, Agile Project Management requires leaders that are quick to think of their feet. This means that you should be able to improve if conditions change in one way or another during the implementation without losing momentum for the team.

The agile method requires you to make decisions that would greatly affect the project later on and you have to make that decision ASAP. If you are the one that tends to linger on the decision making process, then perhaps the Agile Method is a bit too fast for you.

However, you can counteract this by decentralizing the decision making process and sharing it with your team. Perhaps they can come up with a beneficial decision at a rate faster than you can. In addition, this helps in bolstering their trust with the management and ownership with the project. They more they feel that they have a say in the decision-making process, the more motivated they will be in making the agile method sustainable.

Chapter II: The Agile Process

There are two things that should be achieved with the agile project management methodology: shorter production cycles (without sacrificing quality, of course) and more frequent product releases. By having shorter development iterations, a team should be able to react to changes from outside sources more effectively.

As was stated before, there is more than one way to do the Agile method. Scrum and Kanban, for example, feature fairly different work structures from the others. However, each agile methodology follows the basic process which is as follows:

1. Project Planning

Like with any method, you should make the team understand the end goal of the project before starting it. Here, you will explain to them the potential value that succeeding in the project will bring for the team and the company and how it should be achieved.

You may set up a scope for the project here but do not make it unchangeable. The whole premise of the agile method is to adapt to changes that may happen in the middle of the development process. As such, you should avoid getting your team stuck on achieving goals through a static work frame.

2. Creating the Product Roadmap

A roadmap maybe a buzzword for tech guys right now but it is a rather simple yet vital concept to software development. To put it simply, it is a breakdown of what features will make up the final product.

What makes it crucial to the development process as the roadmap tells your team what to focus on in each phase. Also, at this point, you will set up the product backlog which will list all the features and deliverables that will be included in the final product. When you plan for iterations in the future, your team can refer to this backlog to identify what to focus on.

3. Planning Releases

In traditional project management methodologies, there is only one implementation date that comes after the entire project has been developed. However, in the agile method, your project will have a shorter development cycle with features released at their ends.

Before you start the project, you should make a high-level plan for feature releases. And when beginning a new cycle, you shall revisit and re-assess the release plan for those new features.

A high-level plan is basically one that provides a manager's view of the project in its entirety. It's not just a detailed plan where all the tasks required for project completion are indicated. A high level plan includes information on what needs to be done, who is supposed to do the task that needs to be done, how it is done, and when things are expected to be done. This plan is developed with the goal of making sure that progress can be tracked over time.

4. Planning Cycles

Before starting each cycle or iteration, the shareholders need to plan with your team on what shall be accomplished in each segment. Of course, this will also include how such things shall be achieved and how much of a task load should each member of the development carry.

At this point of the process, it is important that you make sure that the load is shared evenly amongst members. This way, they can efficiently accomplish each of their assigned tasks per iteration.

Also, you will need to document your workflow visually. This is to make the task assignment process as transparent as possible to your team and to prevent bottlenecking from occurring when implementing the schedule.

5. Regular (Ideally Daily) Meetings and Correspondence

In order to make your teams accomplish their tasks more efficiently in each cycle, or assess what needs to be improved on, you have to make a habit out of holding short meetings every day. During these meetings, every member will be given the chance to talk briefly as to what they have accomplished for that day and will they be working on in the next.

But it is important that you **keep this meetings short**. Spend no more than 15 minutes in talking with your team as these meetings are not meant for extensive problem solving or chances to talk about things that everybody else has already settled or know of. In fact, you can even do these meetings standing up.

6. Cycle Reviews and Retrospectives

At the end of each iteration, the team will hold two major meetings. In the first major meeting, you will do a cycle review with the client and the shareholders to present to them what has been achieved. And not only are you going to present a sustainable feature, you are going to show to these people a working product.

This is a rather important meeting as it bolsters the communication lines between your team, the shareholders,

and the clients as well as allowing them to give an input which could help in the next iterations.

The second major meeting is the Cycle Retrospective. Here, you and the shareholders will discuss the things that went well during that cycle, what didn't, and whether the work load may have been too heavy or too small for the team. Of course, this meeting will also focus on identifying recurring problems that should be dealt with in the next few iterations, if any.

If you and your team is relatively new to the whole agile project management concept, it is important that you do not skip on these meetings. These meeting would help you determine the task load that your team can handle in each iteration as well as the most effective length for each.

What is the Agile Mindset?

In order to properly implement this methodology, it is important that you and your team have to change your mindset. To do this, you must adopt some values that are necessary for the success of the methodology:

- **Client Satisfaction is at the Top**

The needs of the client must be put first. As such, you must make it a goal to regularly produce content that is functional and of good quality in a timely manner.

When you present progress to a client, they must be able to test it for themselves and come to the conclusion that it is good. They must also be given the chance to air out their concerns and input for the project while also being assured that their concerns are duly noted and will be applied to the best of your abilities.

- **Adaptiveness and Improvisation**

Changes can happen at any time during the process. Even last-minute changes can occur which would ultimately affect the quality of the product. Despite this, you and your team must be accepting of change in any form it takes and adjust your efforts to meet the new goals and conditions.

For leaders, this comes with the extra requirements of being fast enough to act on sudden changes and make important decisions as quickly as possible. The less they mull over what to do next, the more responsive the team will be in addressing sudden shifts in project conditions and goals.

- **Fast Development Cycle**

The ultimate goal of the agile method is to optimize your time. In essence, you and your team should make it a point not to waste time by focusing on the most important goals for each iteration.

Of course, this should mean that each stage of iteration of the development process should be as short as possible.

However, you must be always ready to show results and the progress you have made when clients, shareholders, and management would demand of them in the end of each iteration.

If you have noticed, these three qualities basically summarize the Agile Project Management methodology. They are not exactly written in stone but, as the method itself states, this is the best strategy that you can use to adapt to changes instantly without losing sight of the overall goal.

Also, if certain aspects of your methodology do not work out as planned, you can always make improvements until you see the desired results.

All in all, with the methodology, you should produce three things: a good product, a timely delivery of the same, and a really satisfied client.

Chapter III: Skills, Software, and Organizational Hurdles

A key component in implementing the agile methodology in your project is learning how you can do it. After all, a method is just as good as the tools and implements it offers at your disposal.

Fortunately for you, the agile method is not just about a fancy system of getting things done fast. In fact, you are all the better for the system if you identify what you can do and what you can use to implement the method in your own team.

What are the Key Agile Skills?

Aside from the agile methodology being dependent on the tools that you use, it is also dependent on the people implementing it. Project managers like you should possess certain qualities to make the method effective and sustainable.

A. Ability to Prioritize

At a glance, every task that could be involved in a project seems to be essential. Although this might be true, a project manager knows how tasks are to cut out so that everybody could focus on what is important now.

The project under the methodology, after all, is going to be divided into various iterations. This means that some tasks are not yet important until their corresponding phase arises or, due to the segmentation of the work, are deemed redundant. Your ability to identify what work matters and what is unnecessary will then be crucial for this method.

B. Calm Under Pressure

A project manager using the agile method should have the ability to keep calm under pressure and make crucial decisions even under tremendous stress.

You have to remember that changes are meant to be uncomfortable. Once everybody has settled into a pace or have mentally prepared themselves to do one thing, the last thing that they want to hear is that the rules have changed.

As a project manager, you should be able to handle changes, even last-minute ones, and adjust the work of your team accordingly. In this aspect, you might even have to develop your diplomacy skills to deal with the eventual dissent coming from your team.

C. Coaching Skills

One of the key principles of the agile method is to have a motivated team. The problem with motivation is that it does not exactly last long on its own. You as a leader should be able to keep your team motivated enough to finish each iteration of the development process. You should give them the assurance that everything is still according to plan and, if they are not, you are there to help them transition to the new status quo.

And aside from motivating your team, you should also be able to enhance their skills and guide them through their work without heavy hand-holding. In essence, your leadership should make sure that your team's skillsets and abilities are not the same at the end of an iteration. The more dynamic and expansive the team's combined skillsets are, the more capable it will be in handling challenges that might pop up in the process.

D. Organizational Skills

As a leader, it is your goal to make sure that everyone is doing their share of the entire workload. Aside from prioritizing what needs to be done, you need to be able to remind everyone of deadlines for each iteration.

A major flaw with the agile method, after all, is that it is easy to lose track of the overall goal especially if the iterations are long and numerous. It is your role, then, as a leader to remind everyone that everything that they do must not only contribute to the success of that iteration but to the overall project.

E. Quick Thinking

The ability to make important decisions is a major highlight in the agile method. Project managers then should be able to make rapid changes when the need arise without losing the momentum they have already built for the team.

This means that you should be able to drop strategies at a moment's notice no matter how strongly you feel for that tactic. You must understand that changes are there for a reason and you have to respond by making the necessary adjustments to your schedule. And keep in mind that some decisions have some time limit to them. If you take too long in mulling over your thoughts, you might lose valuable opportunities which results in some periods of inactivity for the rest of the team.

F. Adaptability

Accepting change should start from the leadership. As such, you should be the first to welcome the prospect of changing conditions in the development process.

When you are the first to adapt, you are actually helping the team adapt to the changes as well. This should reduce confusion in the implementation process while also preventing a further breakdown of communications.

But being adaptable is not going to help you if you relay the need for change as quickly as possible. You have to make your team understand why there is a need for changes and demonstrate to them that such changes do not negatively affect the entire iteration but, instead, would enhance the quality of their work.

Management Software

Anyone who wishes to use the Agile Method should also find the corresponding software for it. These programs come with features and systems that make implementation of the agile process possible and, in some cases, easier. Here are some of the Agile-optimized software that you could use for your project.

1. Planbox

One of the most important parts of the agile method cycle is what are called burndown charts (more on this later on). Planbox is a program that can track down these charts so everybody in the team has an accurate idea as to how far (or near) the team is in achieving a certain goal.

The program also integrates features like customer feedback, bug reports, fixes, and other user-generated content that can help you improve on your end product. It also comes with evaluation tools that should make your periodical reviews and retrospective more comprehensive.

Lastly, the program comes with an advanced reporting system that allows you to easily review the status of problem areas in each iteration. And the best part is that Planbox is absolutely free in the market right now.

2. LeanKit

If you are attempting to implement the Kanban variant of the agile method, then this program is the most suitable for you. One of the major features of this program is a live reporting feature where users can post work items and have the same addressed in real time.

This is ideal if your team is not physically together in one workplace. Perhaps you have remote teams working in other areas which makes daily meetings near impossible. But with

LeanKit, in-team correspondence is easier which should make sure that everyone involved in the project is on the same page.

Aside from a live posting and reporting system, LeanKit is also optimized for cross-team platforms and is great for keeping track of dependencies. The program can also be made compatible for Scrum work frames.

The entire program can cost you in between $20.00 and $30.00 per month.

3. Jira

Built from the ground up for the Agile methodology, Jira is often considered to be one of the more dependable project management operating systems out there. It has a rather robust set of features that could help you track, monitor, and even communicate with the rest of your teams through each iteration of the process.

The only major flaw with Jira is that it can be intimidating for newcomers to the agile methodology. It can be complex to use at times and the act of merely setting it up for your workplace will require the help of an experienced developer.

Aside from this, Jira can be expensive. The solutions it offers and the services offered by the team can set up any company by at least thousands of dollars every year. If you are part of a small tech startup, then Jira might not be the best solution for you. Just yet.

Despite these flaws, Jira is rather excellent when it comes to tracking and addressing bugs, and inter-team correspondence. It also has various custom fields that allow you to make the program fit the specifications of your current projects.

4. GIthub Project Management

This program's main selling point is that it is the largest hosted GIt-based server in the market right now. So, you may ask, what does that do for your agile project management method? The answer is that the server allows all your developers to store all code done in projects that have been already finished.

This means that you don't have to rework code you've already done for new projects which can cut the development time by a considerable degree. And the best part is that it can record edits done in real time which means that work can continue where it was left in case of emergencies.

One of the great features of the GIthub program is that it can integrate many other tools for different people involved in the project. There a panel dedicated to developers, another for product owners, another for project manage3rs, and so on and so forth. Your development team can even set up a private communication channel or a public one dedicated to improving code.

The end result is that your team will always have access to the best versions of codes that they have already worked with which should keep work momentum at a high. Pricing for this management program starts free with a $21.00 per user monthly subscription fee if you want access to more features.

5. Clickup

If you have been looking for the most ideal agile management program, then Clickup might be the answer for you. A core feature within Clickup is a feature-driven management program that allows teams to get on top of what needs to be done per iteration while making sure that their efforts contribute to the larger end goal.

Clickup gives users the ability to see an overview of tasks that were completed, yet to be completed, works in progress, and dependencies. With this, you can at the very least prevent tasks from bottlenecking your entire team.

Some of the other features provided by the program include the ability to create epics and set up story points, analyze iteration progress in real time, give users access to custom templates and statuses for process management, time tracking, and other tools that could help in daily meetings.

The best part with Clickup is that it has a Free Forever plan. What this means is that you can get a hold of a copy of the system for absolutely free. However, for access to even more comprehensive features as well as maintenance costs, the program will ask for a $9.00 per month subscription fee for every person that will use the program.

Identifying Organizational Problems

In order for the agile method to work, the entire team must adhere to its principles. This is why the biggest challenge that you would face in implementing the system in your organization is the organization itself. As a matter of fact, there are a number of inherent problems that could impede you from fully enjoying from the agile method if not properly addressed.

A. The Culture

Not every company and team culture out there supports or is even compatible with the agile method. And even if your team is immediately on board to the process, there is the chance that the higher-ups are not so welcoming of it.

This is where a lot of diplomacy should come into play as you have to convince the people that you directly report to that there are benefits to be had from the agile system in order to support it. You have to see things from their perspective in order to do this.

Perhaps the management feels that they are giving away too much independence to your development team and are afraid that this would disrupt internal communications. Or perhaps they have mere misconceptions about the methodology.

Whatever the case, you can actually do a lot on your part to dispel their fears about the system so they would support your project across the different iterations.

B. Unclear Understanding of The System's Impact

In order to get the best results from the agile method, it is not enough that you just implement the systems and tools at your disposal. More often than not, blindly following the principles without reconciling it with the company's goals can result in you wasting time, effort, and money.

Aligning the system with the company's goals and values will still matter as this helps the rest of the company understand why you have to do your project in different iterations. If your team and the rest of the company understands how the Agile method can positively affect the entire organization, you can be certain that the system becomes sustainable in the long run.

C. A Tendency to Rush

One fatal flaw of the agile method is that it taps into man's annoying tendency to rush things through. In the hopes of getting things done fast and in massive quantities, the brain tends to overlook key details.

This results in teams getting focused on getting things done ASAP while missing the most simple and manageable aspects of the development process. This can lead to serious repercussions later on as problems set up in previous iterations can pop up in later ones.

As such, project managers must find a way to keep everyone focus while maintaining the pace of work. In essence, you serve as the first and last line of defense against your team becoming reckless in the development process.

D. Limited Resources

Although agile is quickly becoming popular across the market now, it also means that resources for project managers are still limited now. It can be rather hard to find good talent that can help you implement the method in your team.

However, that does not mean that implementing the system on your own is not entirely impossible. You can start without any mentor for your team and then just look for one once everything has been put in place. And even if you do not find consultants and mentors in your area, you can still make your team generate the best possible results. All that is needed is for you to get the basics of the methodology right.

Chapter IV: The Agile Software Development Process

There is actually no single methodology out there that can work for every project. However, there is no doubt that many development teams and companies are slowly doing away with the more predictive and restrictive methodologies like Waterfall and embracing something more adaptive like Agile.

In fact, you might be surprised that methodologies like Agile were born primarily out of a frustration on how things were used to be done back then. By giving the team much more control over how things are done and for how long, the theory is that the end product will be a far more comprehensive software while still staying true to the client's original vision.

With that, you can easily understand that the Agile process will follow a considerably different development path than conventional and traditional methodologies.

How Development was Done Before

So what was the development process in methodologies like, say, Waterfall? What would be discussed in the next few paragraphs might be elementary to long-time developers. However, it is still necessary that we make a distinction over predictive methodologies over adaptive ones.

The conventional software development process will involve six phases which are as follows:

1. Planning

Obviously, every development process starts with you laying down the specifications of the project. Here, the flow of work will be identified and segmented into smaller and more manageable parts.

The functionalities of each segment and element will also be identified as well as the schedule for each phase of the project. Lastly, workload will be identified here as well as the roles that each member of the development team would perform.

2. Analysis

This part will involve the identifying of goals as well as setting the scope for the entire project. This is a far more detailed process than the planning phase as each stage of the project will be scrutinized.

A major focus on this phase is identifying the allocation of resources for each part of the project. What is the budget for each phase? What are the tools and programs needed? Is there a need to outsource work or hire entirely new people for the job (even temporarily)? These questions need to be sufficiently answered at this part of the process.

Of course, this process will also involve identifying potential issues that might pop up in the middle of the project. In turn, this allows managers to come up with solutions to prevent such from happening.

3. Design

Once planning and analysis have been completed, the team can move on to designing the product. This is a purely conceptual phase as you and your team would visualize what the project looks like by setting up its framework.

Here, the standards for each phase of the project will be established. As such, the team knows what they have to do in order to produce the desired software while also eliminating flaws.

4. Development and Implementation

This is the phase where the product is actually being built. Depending on the chosen methodology, this phase will involve multiple processes which include code writing and the implementation of programming tools and languages.

Once the software is developed, the implementation process kicks in where it goes through various studies and experimentations to see if it, at the very least, functions without crashing.

5. Testing

Once the basic structure of the software is finished, it will then go through a series of tests. Here, the goal is to identify bugs and glitches embedded into the code through the development process and then to fix them.

Like the development process, this is a rather extensive phase as the program has to be scrutinized in all of its aspects and functions to see if it is fit for mass production and distribution.

The most important aspect to be tackled here is determining whether or not the product meets the criteria set in the initial phases of the project. In some cases, the overall layout of your program would be changed in order to address inherent flaws.

6. Maintenance

Prior to mass production, the team should then systematically scour the code for any bugs or glitches that were not identified and addressed in the previous phases.

This part also includes updates that would be introduced way after the product has been released. Patches to the code to address issues or enhance the functionality of the base product.

Flaws in the Conventional Method

Almost all predictive methodologies follow the sequence as laid out above. However, some methods like Waterfall would like to add a few more steps in between such as Research and Feedback.

Whatever the case, predictive methodologies tend to follow a strict sequence in order to create a product that works. However, that does not mean that it is applicable in all cases.

As a matter of fact, there are flaws inherent to these methodologies which may make them inapplicable to your project or, better yet, inferior to other more adaptive methodologies.

1. Restrictive Nature

At a glance, predictive methodologies are so rigid that you have no other option but to follow the plan as was established in the earlier phases. Of course, this means that you are not exactly responsive to changes as they occur in the middle of the project.

In the end, you will produce something that might meet the criteria of the project but does not take into consideration developments that newly occurred. In short, the product might be good if made in restrictive methods but it could have been better.

2. Late Testing

These methods often put the testing process late in the project. This means that the identifying and fixing of bugs is not as comprehensive as you would like them to be. After all, if everything has a set deadline and follows set protocols, you are merely finding and fixing surface-level problems; not inherent, program-breaking ones.

This is where adaptive methods are superior as the testing phase is evenly spread out across all iterations. Simply put, you are correcting your mistakes as you are building the base product.

3. Client Feedback Not Impactful

In most restrictive methodologies, client feedback is often ignored. And if they do acknowledge client feedback, these do not have much of an impact in the development process.

For instance, a client might want to add something to the product during the Feedback and Testing portion.

Depending on how big that change is, it may be ultimately ignored so as not to change the structure of the product or haphazardly applied that it ultimately ruins the quality of the software.

4. High Risk

Since these methodologies are so rigid in their application, you run the risk of not addressing major problems in the coding or add enhancing features until it is too late.

Also, there is a chance that you would have to deal with constant crunch periods as deadlines for each phase are tightly set one after another. As a result, the workload of your team increases along with the pace of work. As such, you run the risk of bottlenecking your project to the point that that end product is haphazardly completed.

The Agile Process Cycle

The process of implementing the agile method differs from one strategy to another. However, they all follow roughly the same sequence, which is:

1. **Conceptualization** – Here, the product is being visualized and designed. The framework for the project will be set up and segmented which helps in prioritizing what needs to be done. Issues like the

allocation of resources and the distribution of workload will also be tackled here.

2. **Inception** – Once the project has been conceptualized, the manager must then focus on building the team (if it does not exist yet, of course). Here, the roles of each team member will be identified while the initial workloads and requirements will be designated to them.

3. **Iteration and Construction** – The most extensive part of the project, this process involves the teams going through each "sprint" or iteration as they build the product. The goal here is to present something that meets the criteria established in each iteration to upper management, shareholders, and the client.

   Since the agile method is iterative by nature, it is necessary that the team goes through each of the set iterations and finish them according to the set time. At the same time, the product that they are building on must grow and develop to meet new standards and other last-minute changes per cycle.

4. **Release** – Once the base product is ready, it will undergo further Quality Assurance checks. This is where major bugs are fixed while the overall layout and user experience of the product will be revamped or enhanced.

This process will also internal and external testing, documentation of what has been fixed, and the final release of the iteration into mass production.

5. **Production** – At this phase, the developers should provide ongoing support for the software. This includes further testing and maintenance as well as the introduction of patches to the code, if need be.

   This should serve as an extra "cycle" to the process where the product is enhanced even if it has already passed the mass distribution phase. Your team can even build on the product's base features by adding more while keeping the code as functional as possible.

6. **Retirement** – Eventually, that product will reach the end of its lifespan, which lasts a year or a few after release. At this phase, the team should initiate some end of product life activities like notifying users of what is to come next and preparing them to migrate to the new product.

The sequence above presents the entire life cycle of products made using the agile model. In fact, there can be more than one agile-centric projects occurring in the same company or multiple iterations being logged in on different product lines. Better yet, the model allows a company to cater to different customers, internal or external, with their own range of needs that need to be met.

The Iteration Workflow

The agile process is dominating by cycles and iterations. Each segment of the project that is completed will actually build on the end product. In essence, with the agile method, you not only have a functional program in each iteration but also supporting features, documentation, and a code that can be used for future projects.

Iterations usually last between 2 weeks and a full month with a fixed period for completion. Since it is time-bound, the process is meant to be methodical and the scope is limited to what must be done in each iteration.

It is not uncommon for a project to have 3 to 10 iterations, depending on its size and type. Each iteration will also follow its own workflow, which can be visualized as follows:

A. **Requirements** – Here, the specifications of the iteration will be set. These must be based on the backlog for the product, the backlog for each cycle, and the feedback of customers and shareholders, if any.

B. Development – At this phase, the team develops or builds upon the software based on the goals set for that segment.

C. Testing – This phase will include Quality Assurance tests, internal and external training, and documentation of what has been improved or developed.

D. Delivery – Once the product is functional, it will then be integrated to make it cohesive. After this, the iteration of the product will then be sent for mass production.

E. Feedback – Once it is in the market, the development team will then monitor how the software is being received by the end users. Are there major flaws that need addressing? What bugs did the team miss but the customers noticed? Is there are a way to improve on the user experience? These questions can be answered at this point of the cycle.

Once the feedback phase is completed, the cycle begins anew with the team conceptualizing on what needs to be done next for the new iteration. The beauty of the method is that you can come up with a better product or an entirely new offshoot in a short period of time.

What are Product Backlogs?

The most basic definition of product backlogs is that they are a list of features that can be added to an existing software created in a previous iteration. And aside from new features, backlogs can include infrastructure changes, bug fixes, and other activities that is necessary to deliver a specific outcome in a current iteration.

In other words, a product backlog answers this question:

"What can we do to make this software Better?"

Aside from the project manager, the product backlog functions as an authoritative source of what needs to be done per iteration. This means that if a task, a feature, or a fix is not on the backlog, then the development team should not even think about investing an iota of effort in performing such a task.

However, the presence of a task on a backlog does not give the assurance that the same can be delivered exactly at the end of that iteration. It only presents the team with an option on how to deliver something that was already promised at the start of the project. It is not a mandatory task that you and your team should commit to.

For example, you and your team might be working on a videogame like, say, a massive multiplayer online role-playing game (or an MMORPG for the sake of convenience). Perhaps your product backlog would include the following:

- Increase item and weapon drops

- Expand on existing world maps

- Add new maps

- Balance skills and classes players discovered to be over-powered

- Fix game-crashing bug on Zones X3 and F10

- Improve chat-based communications

- Introduce Player vs. Player mode

Now, at a glance, you can determine for yourself which of the items must be added ASAP and what could be put off for the next few iterations. The point is that the backlog gives your team an idea as to what should be improved in the next iterations so the overall product is better.

The best part about product backlogs is that you can add on them the more the product is expanded on. The addition of new features to a software gives rise to new opportunities and problems.

However, do rein in your team a bit when it comes to finishing the backlog. There is no rule that your team should clear off that backlog in each iteration. In fact, some of the items in that backlog can be introduced as entirely new features in the next project, depending on the situation.

Burndowns

Arguably, the thing that you have to deal with the most in any project is time. To be specific, you have to make sure that the progress your team is making is sufficient enough to cover the entire time period for that iteration.

And there is this fact that people outside of the development team that want you to finish your tasks *yesterday*. Their intention, after all, is always this: get things done and fast.

As such, it is the job of project managers to understand that time is an element that they must proficiently control in every project that they take. The better data they have when it comes to time in relation to the work that needs to be done, the better a manager can make sure that their team sticks to the approved schedule.

This is where a burndown chart comes into play as it tells how much needs to be done and how much of time has been consumed by the team so far. A burndown chart is simply a graphical representation of how quickly your team is working through a customer's project.

How each agile tool comes up with a burndown chart varies but it often draws information from "stories", detailed descriptions of features of a program as provided by an end-user or the project manager.

So, how do You Read It?

Burndown charts are actually rather simple graphs. The amount of work remaining is always shown on a vertical axis while the time that has elapsed since the start and the projected end of an iteration is drawn horizontally.

The X-axis, the one that represents the timeline is always at a straight line since the period is set. However, the y-axis representing the work that has been done or needs to be completed might fluctuate from day to day. As such, you only need to read the graph from left to right.

But, of course, the more pressing question that you might have with the chart is "what is the ideal burndown trend?" To answer that question, you have to look for certain elements in your reading.

- **Ideal Work Remaining** – The ideal trend for this part should be a straight line connecting from the starting point to the current one. This is a telltale sign that each task has been sufficiently performed and there are no goals that have been untouched as of that iteration.

Also, at the end point, the y-axis line should cross with the x-axis. This indicates that no work is left undone.

- **Actual Work Remaining** – But, of course, it is not exactly easy to pull off a flat line when it comes to graphs. Changes in your work plan can cause some shifts in that graph, resulting in spikes of activity in every point of the chart.

So how are you going to make this work? The best actual trend in this situation is for the actual work line to never go above the ideal work line. If the actual work line does go above the ideal, it is an indication that more work is left undone than originally planned. To put it simply, your team is way behind schedule.

But if the actual work line is below the ideal, then it tells you that your team is actually finishing their tasks on time or, better yet, you are completing the iteration way ahead of the schedule.

To Summarize

So far, we have been discussing how the agile methodology is different from other development methods in relation to how it works and what you need in order to pull it off properly. The point is that you can yield considerable results in your team using this method provided that you get the basics of it right and be constantly proactive when it comes to sudden changes in the project's plan every iteration.

However, there is more than one way to implement the methodology on your project. For the next few chapters, we shall go about how the Agile Method can be carried out by your team through its different frameworks.

Chapter V: The Basics of Scrum

It is important that we talk about the framework that is closely related to the Agile Project Management Method: *Scrum*.

What is Scrum exactly and how do you implement it in your projects? If you have been in the development business for quite a while, you might have heard of this term. You might even have heard it used interchangeably with Agile.

But make no mistake, Agile and Scrum are two different things altogether. Agile is the methodology. Scrum, on the other hand, is the framework wherein that methodology can be implemented.

What Makes Scrum Different?

As its own standalone agile framework, there are a lot of things that make Scrum rather distinct from its siblings.

For starters, time in Scrum is divided into periods called "sprints". They last in between 2 to 4 weeks and, at the end of each sprint, a demonstration of the product as it has been built or improved on will be provided to the client, the upper management, and the shareholders.

At a glance, Scrum is the methodology that is the most at home in teams that already adopt a mindset focused on product development. However, that is not to say that it can't be made to be compatible with other teams, especially those that are relatively new to the entire agile process.

This is not the only way that Scrum is fundamentally different. Here, there are no projects with definite start and finish dates, giving the development full rein as to when they would present a product at the end of the iteration.

Another difference is the hierarchy of management. In Scrum, there is no singular project manager. In fact, there is no project manager necessary to tell people what to do, when to do it, and when it must be submitted.

Instead, in Scrum, the team decides when to deliver improvements to a product over a period with which they are most comfortable. As such, Scrum has the most decentralized decision-making body amongst all project management methodologies right now, even among Agile-based variants.

Lastly, Scrum is not that particular with upfront planning. In this framework, teams can adjust their work according the feedback of clients and shareholders while keeping the pace that they have set for that sprint.

The Principles of Scrum

As with other project management methodologies, Scrum's framework is based on several foundational concepts. If you want to succeed in implementing this framework, then you should adhere to the following principles.

A. **Self-Organization** – The team should never think that they are doing this project because someone is telling them so. To come up with a product that they can identify with, they should have some sense of autonomy over how to do things and what to include.

To put it in other words, a project tends to be more successful if the people making it identify themselves with it more. This includes being free to determine who does what and when things should be delivered.

B. **Delivering Value** – Teams should be focused on delivering value for each iteration. So what does value look like under the Scrum framework? The most basic answer to that is an improved product.

Simply put, the product should have expanded and grown by leaps and bounds for every iteration it goes through. If it was mediocre and basic in the first iteration, then it should be better and expansive in the next, and more comprehensive in the succeeding sprints.

C. Collaboration – Cross functionality is a major concern that needs to be addressed under this framework. Essentially, they should be able to assist their own team members in identifying problems and then finding solutions around them.

It is important that each team member knows what they can contribute to the entire effort and what role they must play in the overall project. Also, they must be able to motivate others in completing tasks on time or, better yet, way ahead of the schedule.

D. Time – Sprints are meant to be short bursts of activity that allow teams to produce something within the time period. As such, the leader must find a balance in keeping the team focused on getting the job done on time without pressuring them to meet a deadline.

The point here is that the team should be fast and efficient in their work but without adopting a deadline-focused mindset in the project.

E. Iteration and Improvement – The team must make it a point to improve on the product in every iteration. When they ship it, they have to wait on the feedback. And, depending on the feedback they received, they will plan their next sprint so as to enhance the product even further. Rinse and repeat.

Why Should You Use It?

What is the point of using this framework, if there is any? The truth is that the Scrum does offer some benefits for those that implement it. They are the following:

Better Team Morale – Ownership over a project is what separates a Scrum team from other development teams. Since they have a say in how things are done, then they have more a personal stake in the project's success.

Thus, a scrum developer go out of their way to contribute to the entire effort to the best of their abilities. To put it simply, if they have a say in what the team's success should look like, they are more empowered. And an empowered team tends to bring in more than 100% of their effort every day.

Fewer Risks – Conventional project management will involve a lot of heavy-handed planning at the start of the project. This is basically the time when everybody else knows the least of what they are going to build.

As such, planning in this stage is rather risky as teams have to figure out what the end goal is. And then there is the fact that changes in technology can happen mid-process which increases the chances of teams having to do the project all over again.

In Scrum, however, the team can interact with customers and shareholders more efficiently at every stage of the development process, especially the earlier ones. As a direct result, the chances of the product being a poor fit for the market where it is to be distribute and it being negatively affected by sudden shifts in technology are at least minimized.

A Better Product – A key feature in Scrum is the ability to ship out a working product in a short period of time. By shortening product cycles, the team can get hold of customer feedback at a faster pace. In fact, you can get the input that you need as soon as they are created in real time.

Thus, you have a system that allows you to improve on what has been shipped on a constant basis. This way, your team creates an ultimate expression of the client's vision faster and more efficient than in any other development frameworks.

3-4-5

All these talks of Scrum can look complicated, but it is actually rather simple to follow. In fact, you can break the framework even further into a set of 3 roles, 4 "artifacts", and 5 events.

All in all, these elements form a structure that is responsive to feedback and is more than able to go to toe with an increasingly unpredictable trend in development in recent years. It sounds simple, right? And it can be made even simpler.

1. 3 Roles

The Scrum Framework only utilizes 3 roles for the entire project which are as follows:

A. **The Scrum Master** – The scrum framework might do away with the project leader or manager but it does need a coach. This is where the scrum master comes into play as they facilitate the implementation of the process.

The role of the scrum master is rather straightforward. They are primarily there to remove potential impediments in the flow of information and resources and make sure that everyone is working according to the pace they have agreed to at the start of the project. They are not there to tell everybody what to do but to make sure that they are doing what they have agreed to perform.

Another role that the scrum master performs is ensuring that the work of the team remains uninterrupted. This means that they also act as liaison for the team with upper management, shareholders, and stakeholders while also acting as a "lightning rod" in case disputes arise. By dealing with outside interruptions, the scrum master makes sure that the team can focus on delivering on their promises in every iteration.

B. The Product Owner – This person serves as the proxy of the client to the team. He is the one primarily responsible for conveying the vision of the client to the team to guide them on what to do for each iteration.

AS such, the product owner sets the standards for the project by prioritizing the product backlog (one of the artifacts of the Scrum method), preparing the criteria for acceptance, and approving of items at the end-of-cycle review.

The product owner is not someone that needs to be tech-savvy in order to be effective in this role. However, they do need to have a good grasp of what customers perceive to be acceptable in a product. They also should have an understanding of the competition, trends in the market, and other outside elements that could affect the overall reception of the product.

In essence, the product owner is there to remind everyone involve that the vision must be upheld first and foremost. This should guide the developers in determining how to adapt to sudden changes in the market and what must be done in the next few iterations.

C. **The Scrum Team** – The team is the one primarily responsible for, well, developing the product through every iteration it goes through. For software projects, a team would usually include engineers, architects, programmers, quality assurance experts, testers, and programmers.

In each sprint, the scrum team is responsible for identifying the kind of goals they must accomplish from the artifacts and choose the method of which they are to meet the goals. They also have full autonomy over how things are done in each cycle but would still have to rely on the guidance of the scrum master and product owner.

2. 4 Artifacts

The Scrum framework is dependent on several artifacts that dictates the specifications of the project. Combined, these artifacts tell the project team what needs to be done, where it goes, who handles on the team, and when.

A. **The Product Backlog** – This is a list of prioritized deliverables that should be implemented as part of the project or a specific iteration. This artifact is important for decision-making sessions as they help the team understand what needs to be done or what might become important in the future.

In other words, the product backlog helps in ensuring the team works on the most critical features of the product. This includes fixing bugs, adding new features, and other work that is important to the overall quality of the product.

B. **Product Backlog Items** – What, then, makes up a product backlog? There are actually a wide array of Product Backlog items (PBIs) to choose from. In the realm of software development, however, they are all classified in 4 groups.

The first two groups consists of elements that are easily observed by end users. These are Features and Bugs and it is the role of the development team to improve on the former while minimizing the latter.

The other two, however, are more technical in nature. Thus, they are things that are too complex or invisible to the end user but would nonetheless affect their overall perception of the product. These two classes are Technical Debt and Spikes (information gathered from research that is not code).

PBIs are usually written in what is called a "Story" form. Thus, it could look something like this:

"As a (Insert User here), I want (Insert useful action here) so that (Insert value here) can be achieved".

C. **Sprint Backlog** – This backlog contains work that the team must do now or as part of the 2-4 week sprint. Sprint Backlogs are usually formed during meetings and do not change at all for the duration of the sprint. They also dictate how the team is performing as far as the Burndown chart is concerned.

Sprint backlogs are usually user stories that the team has committed to meeting during that iteration. However, it could also include some issues shared with the product backlog such as fixing bugs, adding features, and restructuring the product.

Unlike the product backlog, which is merely a list of what the user wants, the sprint backlog is a bit more technical. It breaks down what the team must focus on for that sprint and details how the stories can be implemented on a technical level. The Scrum master will refer to this backlog in guiding the rest of the team through the sprint.

D. Increment – This is simply the sum of all the PBIs that have been completed during a sprint. Simply put, it determines if the team is one step closer to achieving the overall vision of the client.

Ideally, at the end of each sprint, the increment placed on each PBI must be "done". This indicates that all tasks set for that cycle have been successfully met and there is no work to be carried over in the next period.

But how can you tell that something is "done"? For software developers, completion simply means that that feature is usable and efficiently implemented into the code of the product. The scrum master, product owner, and the team will then refer to the increment in presenting to outside individuals what has been done so far in achieving the overall goals of the project.

3. 5 Events

The scrum framework has several defined events throughout each project. These events, in turn, combine to give the team the focus they need on providing value to the clients across every iteration. The sequence of events under the scrum framework, then, are as follows:

A. **Sprint Planning** – At the beginning of each sprint, the team convenes for a meeting. Here, the team, master, and owner plan what needs to be done for the upcoming cycle.

It usually starts with the product owner presenting the top priority PBIs and ends with the team committing to a sprint backlog. It is important, however, that the team chooses the items that they are most confident of completing by the end of that sprint.

B. **The Sprint and The Standup** – the sprint is simply the time-fixed period where the team goes about completing the tasks they have agreed to. But, of course, there is a chance that the team might get behind due to some changes or, worse, a lack of supervision.

This is where the **Daily Standup** becomes important. As the name implies, this is a meeting held every day where the scrum master tells the team what to prioritize for that day or for the week. And also as the name would imply, you could do this meeting standing up so keep the meetings short. This way, everybody can get the reminders that they need and get back to work immediately.

C. The Sprint Review

Once the sprint is ending, the scrum master will call for another meeting. Here, he presents the results of what has been achieved to shareholders and the client (if the latter is available, of course).

Ideally, the Sprint Review is where a tangible product must be presented in the form of a demo of an actual working version. This is how the team should showcase what they have achieved for that sprint and to demonstrate that the acceptance criteria that has been set in the start of the sprint has been met.

D. The Sprint Retrospective

Also held at the end of the sprint, this is where the master, owner, and team evaluate several key issues in the current sprint. These include:

- What happened in the current sprint?

- What challenges did each team faced?

- How efficient was the team in achieving the sprint goals?

- What can be improved in the next sprint?

- What should be included as PBIs in the next sprint?

At this retrospective, the development team should focus primarily on what they can do to improve as a group. This means that they ought to put their focus on the things that they have direct control over with like the handling of workloads, scheduling, and the flow of information between persons and sub-teams.

Anything that they cannot handle like corporate policies, client concerns, and pressure from upper management is best left for the Scrum Master and Product Owner.

Chapter VI: Extreme Programming
Part I: The Basics

In practice, the Agile Methodology is highly applicable in all sorts of projects; not just those that involve coding and programming. If you have a project that involves something that needs to be developed prior to mass production, then you can use various Agile frameworks to guide your production and development process. This is irrespective of the fact if that end product has to be made on a work bench or a desktop computer.

However, the Agile was designed primarily for software development and this all the more apparent with its software-focused variant, Extreme Programming (or XP for short). XP is an Agile framework whose core purpose is to improve the quality of the software as well as the work process of which the development team is to adhere to. And if the process and the end product is improved, then needs of the customer are satisfied or more.

Core Principles

Extreme Programming is a framework by nature. As such, its success is utterly dependent on its implementers adhering to 5 basic values which are as follows:

A. Communication – The XP framework demands that the development team maintains an open, transparent, and effective channel of communication within each other and with people outside. The exchange of ideas, concerns, and other crucial information must be so clear and direct so as to minimize confusion and waste of time.

B. Simplicity – Reduction of waste is a strong focus in the XP framework. This, in turn, can only be possible if the team adopts a system that is straightforward and a software design that focuses on the basics. This way, the team can put all their efforts into creating important features, addressing the most pressing of issues, and creating a product that is easy to produce, monitor, and maintain.

C. Feedback – There is no doubt that feedback is integral to creating a good product. However, the XP framework takes things a bit further and demands that feedback be not only constantly given but also immediately acted on. This will help the team quickly identify where they can improve on and make important changes to their development practices.

D. Respect – The XP framework understands that each person in the team plays a crucial role in the success of the project. Thus, their personal needs have to be respected and the members must bond with each other both at a professional and personal level. A more cohesive team will be able to achieve the project's goals quickly and more efficiently.

E. **Courage** – The XP framework encourages everyone involved to be courageous. And by courage, the framework needs everyone to speak out when they feel something is not working or something might negatively affect the quality of the product and the efficiency of the development process. Alternatively, they must be courageous enough to face criticism or feedback of their work and improve on their methodologies accordingly.

When is it Applicable?

Due to the unique nature of the framework, XP is not exactly applicable for all types of projects out there. The general characteristics, principles, and practices promoted by this framework is best appreciated in projects that revolve around or deal with the following:

- **Changing Software Requirements**

  Software development processes were meant to be short because technology changes at a blistering pace especially in recent years. The Videogame Duke Nuke

Forever, for example, was announced somewhere in the mid-1990s but was released in 2011.

Aside from the usual development problems and corporate issues involved, one major element that impeded the game's release was the changing of technology especially with graphics processors. In fact, the game had to be overhauled by no less than 3 times in a span of a decade as graphics engines and corresponding hardware developed quickly especially during the early 2000s.

Moreover, despite all of the efforts and money pooled into the project, the end result was disappointing to many as the conflicting engines and design philosophies ultimately lead to a jumbled mess of a game.

- **Time-Related Risks in Using New Technology**

If a project were to capitalize on a new piece of technology, then it goes without saying that the product needs to be released while that technology is still relevant.

Longer development times run the risk of certain technologies being incorporated in the software being replaced by ones that are more efficient. This means that if such shift were to happen mid-development, then the team has to do everything all over again.

This constant doing-over can cause a lot of time to be wasted as well as production delays. Ultimately, the end product released is but a compromised version of what the client intended in the first place.

- **Small Development Team**

The XP framework was designed to take advantage of smaller development teams. A small development team means that communication lines are smaller, more direct, and easier to manage. It also means that issues get addressed quickly while feedback is near-instantaneous.

This even works across multiple subgroups so as long as they are co-located or are working in the same vicinity.

- **Autonomous Program**

The technology that should be used in the project must allow for automated unit and functional tests. This is because the team should be given the chance to fully focus their efforts on developing the software or improving on existing ones.

Automated tests do speed up the testing and maintaining phase which shortens an already short development period. If incorporated right, the team should have no problems moving from one phase of the project to another.

What's the Advantage of XP?

So what should you expect if you are to apply the XP framework in your projects? The answer to that could be different from one project head to another. However, let us just say that XP is something that is not definite in the advantages that it offers to its users.

What it does offer, however, is the chance to do away with some of software development's more infuriating issues, which include the following:

A. **Slipped Schedules** – With a focus on shorter development schedules, XP allows a project team to deliver something tangible and of value to customers on a regular basis. This also means that they can get to finish tasks on time without overexerting themselves.

B. **Cancelled Projects** – Ultimately, it is client dissatisfaction that kills projects. Whether something gets delayed for several times or the client itself is disappointed with the end result (or a bit of both), there is a high probability that elements in the development process will result in the entire project being canned or put on hold. Either way, everybody wasted their time for something that won't see the light of day.

C. **Change-Induced Costs** – In the XP process, ongoing and extensive testing makes sure that changes are implemented into the program without compromising its base functionality. A running and working system always ensures that changes are accommodated and given enough time and attention at in order to be properly incorporated into the main code.

And the best part is that the team can adjust their work accordingly without losing momentum.

D. **Production and Delivery Defects** – Constant testing and integration will expose flaws and bugs in the design which the team can then address to the best of their abilities. With these tests, the structure of the code is thoroughly cleaned which means that the team can now shift their focus on "enhancing" the product post-launch instead of "fixing" what is inherently wrong with it that users have to discover for themselves.

E. **Misunderstandings** – More often than not, projects result in failure because of a failure of communication. It is either that the customer was never given the chance to constantly communicate or, if they do, the developers never fully understood what the latter wanted out of the project.

By making the customer an actual part of the team, communication is now direct and clearer. If the exchange of ideas and information is faster and more transparent, the end product will be a more accurate reflection of the customer's vision and intention for the project.

F. **Business Changes** – Change is always inevitable but they are often detrimental to the team. After all, there is nothing more damaging to the morale of the entire group than to tell them to start everything over again.

In the XP framework, not only is your team more open towards change. They can also be more anticipative of it. This means that they conduct their work in a manner that allows them shift gears in the instance that they need to do so. And while doing this, the team must never lose sight of the goal which is to complete the vision of the customer to the best of their abilities.

G. **Constant Staff Turnover** – As a result of delays, technical issues, and interpersonal conflicts, a team's roster can change frequently which affects the quality of the end product. The XP framework puts a strong focus on team collaboration and communication with external people.

On paper, this should promote transparency and goodwill with everyone involved in the project. If everyone identifies with the project and has a strong sense of ownership over it, they can contribute 100% of their effort in completing the project.

XP in Practice

Aside from values and principles, the XP framework is dependent on you adopting new practices. These practices, in fact, were made to be interconnected with each other through the framework provided by XP. They are the following:

1. **The Planning Game** – XP addresses two key questions in software development: what must be done before a due date and what needs to be done next? The emphasis, then, is on directing the project instead of predicting what needs to be done and how long. As such, the Planning Game can be done in two strategies.

A. Release Planning – Here, the customer presents the desired feature to programmers who, in turn, estimate how it should be done and how difficult each feature is to incorporate. With cost estimates at hand and with knowledge of how important each feature is, the Customer essentially laws out the project. All that the development team has to do is to follow the specifications and produce the desired results to the best of their ability.

However, release plans may change and those project estimates are never definite. Even if the initial release plan is manageable, the XP team must revise the plan regularly to fit in changing development conditions.

B. Iteration Planning – In this strategy, the team is given direction of what needs to be done every two weeks. Essentially, the project is divided into what we now know as "iterations".

As this is the more Agile-ready strategy, developers are given the option to determine for themselves what needs to be done for every iteration and commit to completing the same within that time period. The point here is that they must be able to produce something functional at the end of that period.

But what should you and your team talk about when doing planning sessions? Here are a few issues that need to be tackled by the business and management people in the team.

Scope – How much of a problem must be solved in order for the system to be better? The upper management, customer, and the coach are in the position to determine whether or not enough effort has been done to address issues and where the team should focus on next.

Priority – With all the tasks that need to be done, which ones need to be completed first? Yes, the team ultimately decides what they want to do with each task but it is the leaders who should determine what stories are ultimately important to the end product.

Release Composition – How much (or how little) needs to be done before the business improves with the software than without it? This is something that a leader can only determine as a developer's intuition as to how the business is going to benefit from the completion of the project is not as accurate as that of a management-trained person.

Date of Releases – When should the end products be released to the public? And if they are released on that date, would their presence be welcomed in the market or even have a huge impact on it?

The overall impression of the public to the software upon release is something that managers and project heads are more capable of identifying than developers and software technicians.

These are management related issues but what about the more technical stuff? Your development team can also discuss issues that it can handle such as:

Estimates – How long will a feature take to be implemented? This is something that developers can determine based on their combined skill sets and expertise.

Consequence – There are some strategic management decisions that can only be made if the management folk are fully aware of some technical consequences that could arise from such. If strategy A were to be used, what would happen next? And if B was used, what detriment would it serve to the company?

The development people need to explain this to management so they can make better informed decisions in behalf of the entire project.

Process – What is the organization of the team for this project? What is the workload for each member? The team must be a perfect fit not only for the specifications of the project but also the culture for which they are to operate under.

The reason for this is that the end product will reflect the overall cohesion of the team. If the team functions well, then the software should have a stable structure with all of its promised features properly implemented.

Schedule – Within a planned released, what stories should be included? The developers should have the freedom to schedule the most labor intensive and riskiest segments first so as to reduce the overall risk for the entire project.

Of course, this in-team set of priorities must be reconciled with the business's overall priorities for the project. If done so, this reduces the chance of important features being dropped just to meet deadlines.

At a glance, you should realize that the planning process should be a joint collaborative effort by the development team, the business persons like upper management, and the customer.

2. **Small Releases** – In XP, teams do small releases in two different ways. First, the team releases running and tested software to the customer in every iteration. The customer can use this software for any purpose that they have in mind. The goal in this strategy is to give the user something tangible and useful for every iteration.

   The second option is to release something to end users as frequently as possible. This means that an initial product is released and the team continues to build (and fix) that product over a period of time.

3. **Metaphor** – Teams following the Extreme Programming framework must develop a common vision of how the program should look and function which is the "Metaphor". The best definition of this metaphor is that it is an accurate description of what the end product would be like after extensive development has been done on it.

   This metaphor, as the name would imply, does not need to be technical. It can be poetic or it can be dramatic as the framers would like. The point here is that the metaphor is an expression of the vision of the entire team which points them to a general direction when starting a project.

4. **Simple Design** – The XP framework puts a lot of focus on software with a design that is simple but is adequate. The project starts with something simple and, with further programming and testing, ends up with something that is still simple.

As such, the Team must keep the design suited for those conditions. Needless elaboration is a waste of motion which complicates the value of the product.

However, designing is not a one-time affair in XP. It always occurs in the project to meet new needs and address current technological shifts. Also, there are dedicated design phases in each iteration. With this, the software changes for the better in each cycle but stays true to the notion of simplicity.

5. **Testing** – XP is largely focused on feedback which can only be acquired through constant testing. Good XP teams practice what is called as "Test-Driven Development" where they work in short development cycles, add a test run, and make things work.

However, there is a difference between setting up a good test and running it. Your team must do test runs correctly once they release new code to the repository. Also, you have to make sure that the test covers 100% of the new code. This should provide the feedback of which your team relies in determining what needs to be done later on.

6. **Refactoring** – Also known as Design Improvement, this practice focuses on delivering value to the customers in every iteration. To accomplish this over the entire project, your team must abide by the Refactoring process, which focuses on improving several key issues of the design.

    First, the team must detect and remove duplication all over the code, which is a telltale sign of poor software design. After this, the team must then work in improving the cohesion of the entire code and ensuring nothing is fundamentally broken.

    On practice, this allows the team to start with a good and simple software design and build on that in every iteration. This reduces the chances of the team having to start from scratch in every cycle, streamlining the development process even further.

7. **Pair Programming** – All production in the XP framework is built by two programmers who work at the same code at the same time. This should ensure that the code is reviewed, tested, and implemented by

two different people who understand how it works line by line.

The act of letting two people what one can do on their own might sound impractical but programming seems to be the deviation of the norm. Research has shown that paired programmers produce code that is more functional and easier to implement than singular programmers. To put it simply: Two heads are better than one.

Aside from resulting in better code, pair programming also helps in communicating information to the team in a more efficient manner. When working on a shifting basis, every pair involved in the development process can get to learn what the others have been working on and where they specialize in.

The more a programmer learns from their peers, the more valuable they become to the team. In essence, Pair programming helps your team evolve as a self-sufficient group without having to add new talent every cycle.

8. **Collective Ownership** – On an XP project, any pair of programmers can improve on the code on their shift. This means that the code itself gets the

benefit of being attended to by many people, which reduces defects and improves its overall quality.

There is also another, more important, benefit. When everyone has ownership of the code, they are more invested in making it work. Singular ownership of a code can result in features being replaced or written over when a new programmer replaces the old one. The result is that the code becomes too complex or, if functional, a major deviation of the customer's initial vision.

Of course, Collective Ownership can make people work blindly on a code without fully understanding what it must do. This can be easily avoided through tests and constant communication. This way, improvements are delivered when they are requested and everybody on the team share the same knowledge on how to complete the product for each iteration.

9. **Continuous Iteration** – The XP framework is all about optimizing work. In other methodologies, daily builds are seen as irrelevant or, in some cases, weak. But the XP method understands that daily builds are not only integral to producing good product but can be done multiple time in a day.

To understand what this means, think of the software development process as building a car. Each team might work on some part of the vehicle like one team focuses on the engine and transmission while the others focus on the electronics, interior, and fuel intake.

All of their work is necessary to the completion of the product but there is still the challenge of making everything cohesive during the actual process of assembling the car. Some parts might be well made but don't fit the overall design. Some might fit the overall design but could negatively impact the overall functionality.

Software integration faces the same problem. Your team might find that some lines of the code are not compatible with each other or, worse, create bugs in the system. Of course, errors in the system means that your team has to work double the time in fixing them while delivering on the software on the promised date.

With continuous integration, your team can correct on its mistakes as they are made as you make sure that each part complements one another as they are being developed.

This way, the overall software is cohesive and major, program-crashing errors are eliminated before the software gets mass produced. After all, it is easier (and less stressful) to fix problems while the project has not yet been shipped.

10. **The 40 Hour Work Week** – The XP framework directly addresses one of the major criticisms of software development: it's reliance on Crunch Times. What we know as Crunch Times are basically periods in the development process where people have to invest more time in delivering the promised features on a due date.

The XP framework recognizes that crunch times are not only unnecessary, they are detrimental to the health, sanity, and overall wellbeing of the developers. The team must commit to delivering the features on time but they must not over-extend themselves.

In essence, they must give100% of their effort for 8 hours and 5 days of the week. Nothing less and nothing more. This could be done by distributing the tasks over several iterations and making the team prioritize on what needs to be done for that specific iteration.

This way, value is provided in every cycle and your team members are not left severely exhausted at the end of each segment.

11. **The On-Site Customer** – The team using the XP framework must coordinate their efforts with a

representative of the client as closely as possible. This "on-site customer" gives the team an impression of what the end client wants from the project.

Also, they are the tones that primarily test the product at the end of each iteration. Here, they can provide feedback which gives the team an idea as to what to do and improve on the software in the next iteration.

12. **Coding Standard** – IF people work on the code by pairs, how is the XP framework going to ensure its cohesiveness at the end of each iteration? This is done by making the team follow a common coding standard.

Basically, the team must adhere to a set list of principles and specifications when working on the code. These principles and specifications are, in turn, based on the information provided to them by the on-site customer.

By adhering to the standard, the development team can create code written as if only one person has been working on them. The specifics of the standard are not exactly important here. What is more important is that the end code, all of the parts that comprise it, would look familiar in support of the notion of collective code ownership.

Chapter VII: Extreme Programing Part 2: Unifying Practices

Over the years, those that use the XP framework discovered that the 12 practices above often complement one another. For example, a Common Standard in the code helps in reinforcing the idea that everyone has ownership of the end product as a collective. Or the 40-hour work week helps developers prioritize what is important instead of spreading themselves too thin, complementing the practices of simple design, small releases, and refactoring.

But there is always risks entailed in implementing these practices, risks that would otherwise derail the entire project. To eliminate such risks, you must find a way to unify ALL XP Practices and, to do that, there are a few tips that you can keep in mind:

1. **Mind the Team Buildup**

Teams should be comprised of cross-functional subgroups made up of different people with different sets of skills. With this, the team members can complete each other in accomplishing a specific goal for each iteration.

2. **Sit Together**

Most people would agree that conversations done on a face basis are the best form of communication for projects. As such, teams should find a time where they could sit together (or stand) without barriers to direct communication.

3. **Make the Workspace Informative**

The workspace must be arranged in a way that teams can directly work or communicate with one another. If the exchange of ideas and information is unimpeded on a practical scale, the project can be done at a faster pace.

4. **Keep the Work Energized**

Everyone working on the team must be focused on the work at hand, which means that they must be mentally and physically healthy at all times. As such, they should not be overworked by abiding the 40 hour work week schedule. Also, a person must support the need to protect the mental and physical wellbeing of other members.

Roles

Although Extreme Programming is not that strict in making your team adhere to a specific combination of practices, it does not also exactly establish roles for your team to fill in during the development process.

That being said, however, there are certain positions which have popped up across XP teams in different projects. You are not required to follow these roles for your team, mind you, but they should give you an idea as to what task must be done by who in the project.

1. The Customer

This person is responsible for making all the decisions regarding the project. In fact, they are the ones to determine what to do with issues such as:

- What should the end product do?

- What features should be included in it?

- How would the team know that a product is finished? What are the acceptance criteria?

- How much should the team spend? What is the available funding?

- What should the team do for the next iteration?

A customer in the XP framework is required to be actively engaged with the development of the product since they are essentially part of the core team. Of course, there is no law out there that says you can't have more than ONE Customer for every project. Your team can benefit greatly from multiple perspectives so as long as there is a clear direction of what needs to be done.

2. The Developer

Since the XP framework is not particular with role definitions, everyone who is directly involved in building the product is going to be called a "Developer". This does not matter if they are tasked with building the code, testing it, or doing bug fixes.

Developers under the XP framework are the ones primarily responsible for realizing the vision of the Customer. And since every project requires a different set of skills, and because the XP method is reliant on cross-functional team support, those who made the framework felt there was no particular need to lay out the different roles that a developer should take in the project.

What is only necessary is that the skills and expertise they have can complement what others have, resulting in a more cohesive team for the project.

3. The Tracker

Some XP teams find it necessary to include a tracker in their lineup. More often than not, these are the developers who would devote an extra bit of their time every week to fill in this role. The primary purpose of the tracker is to track the metrics relevant to the project and make sure that the team is completing their work on time.

They are also responsible for identifying where the team should improve on in the next iteration. As was stated, this role is not required for your team in every project you take. A tracker is only needed if your team finds it necessary to have someone monitor how everyone is doing in their respective tasks.

4. The Coach

And since we are assuming that this is your first time applying the XP method to your projects, you would need some veteran to guide you through the process. This where the Coach comes into play and he is usually someone who is outside of the team but definitely knows how XP works. As such, it is his role to guide you and your team through the framework and make sure that you are optimizing it on your project.

It is necessary for a Coach to have first-hand experience in handling XP projects. This way, they can guide you through and help the team avoid common mistakes in the framework, some of which they might have personally encountered or have committed in their own experiences.

As was established, the XP framework is not too fussy in you defining roles for the team. Your team lineup might be quite different from the others but would fit the specifics of the project. The point is that you must make sure that each person plays a crucial role in translating a client's vision into a working, bug-free software.

What are the XP Activities?

Regardless of the tasks your team has agreed to per iteration of the XP process, the framework would still require you to do 4 main tasks which forms the entire XP development process. They are the following:

Designing – A good code always starts with a good design. The design is what guides the project through and helps the developers identify what must be included in the project in order to meet customer goals.

When designing a product, the team must make sure that it adheres to the notion of simplicity. The design itself must allow for straightforward coding as unnecessary embellishments only complicate things, leading to more bugs and errors in the final product.

In order to prevent design-based issues, the developers must create a design structure that helps organize logic through its system. Simply put, the flow of information and the interconnection of multiple lines of code must be simple enough that end users can get the hang out of using the product once it is mass-produced and shipped.

A good design also avoids the problem of dependencies in the system. This is where changes made on one code or feature will affect the functionality of the others. If possible, the code structure must allow for a single line of code to be isolated when necessary and its changes do not affect the stability of the rest of the system.

Coding – To those that swear on the effectiveness of XP, the most vital component of the process of developing the software is building the code. Coding is important for laying the groundwork for the transition from a mere idea to a working product.

Here, the development team will go about building the code in pairs. The framework demands that the code must not only be simple and straightforward but shares a unified design regardless of who is currently working on it. The sharing of feedback and addressing of issues is also necessary when integrating the work of the respective programmer pairs into a functional system.

Testing – If a few tests can eliminate flaws in the system, then constant testing can do a lot in cleaning up the entire program and optimizing it. Unit tests must be performed in order to assess which features are working (or not) according to the specifications set.

Acceptance testing is also necessary to make sure that the developers understand the requirements of the project and, in turn, find ways to meet the same with their work.

Developers must also write automated tests to speed this process up without sacrificing accuracy. If all goes well, then the primary code can be regarded as working and complete.

The point here is that every line of code included in the system must be tested and determined to be optimized before moving on to other features.

Listening – This is not exactly a technical process but it is nonetheless necessary in the completion of the project. The development team and manager must take the time to have a sit down with the customer and other individuals to discuss the progress of the project.

Here, they are to listen to whatever concern these people might have especially the ones that delve with the performance of the project. Perhaps there is a perspective here that the team has not yet tapped into or a potential problem that they did not take notice of.

Whatever the case, the customer, shareholder, and upper management have a voice that needs to be heard if the team were to create something that meets their expectations.

The XP Lifecycle

The XP framework espouses the concept of simplicity which is not only limited to the design of the software. This can also be seen in the process and, ultimately, the lifecycle of the project.

First, you must describe the desired results of the project by having the customers define a set of stories. As these stories are being developed, the team estimates the size and requirements for each story.

This estimate along with the relative benefit estimated by the customer will give the team an indication of the relative value of the story. This allows the customer to determine the sequence of stories in the development process according to their priority.

But do keep in mind that not all stories are not easy to estimate which means that they take a bit more time to apply to the system. Of course, there is the chance that they don't fully understand all the technical considerations and specifications it involves. So what is the team supposed to do with them?

In the middle of the development process, they can introduce a "spike" where they can focus on that particular story or feature. Spikes are short, time-boxed time frames that are set aside for the team to do research on something that they don't fully understand.

If you have to put a spike, however, place it in between iterations. This way, your team does not have to drop everything that they have to do just to learn something new.

Once the stories have been settled, the team can then start on creating a release plan based on what they feel is reasonable for the project. This release plan details what stories should be tackled on a specific time period or what is to be released. This way, the team settles on what needs to be done first and then next and next after that. And so on and so forth.

This is then where the concept of Weekly cycles would become important as they help the team stay focused on the tasks at hand. Simply put, the stories must be broken down into tasks for each week. This in turn gives each team member a clear set of what needs to be done for a day or for the entire week, depending on the size of a particular task.

At the end of each week, the team will then do a progress report and review what has been achieved. At this point, the customer has full say on whether or not to continue on the project. If sufficient value has been provided by way of a functioning feature or a revamp of the entire program, the customer can then decide if they want to add more to the end product.

This process goes on and on until the product is ready for mass production. Once the final phase of the development process is reached, the team can then declare the project to be over and move on to a new one.

Chapter VIII: Lean

There are many goals that could be achieved if you are seriously considering applying an agile methodology in your projects. However, if there are one thing agile project managers could agree on what is one of the more important goals to be achieved with the method, it would be an increase in Productivity?

What does productivity look like? That would be different for every development team and project manager. For some, productivity is reflected in a change in inventory management. For others, it is the increase of output while the input is lessened or maximized.

And then for some, productivity is the elimination of waste in the production and development process. And if eliminating waste is an issue that is close to your heart, this is where the Lean methodology would play an important role in your project.

What's the Lean Project Management Method?

Lean is a management philosophy created by Toyota Production System. It is something that has been implemented in Japan for decades now, but it was only in the 1980s when the rest of the world took notice of it.

Simply put, a lot of western companies noticed that their Japanese counterparts were slowly outperforming them. How could a country whose production facilities were leveled by a war just a few decades ago not only rebuild itself but managed to outpace western countries?

Whatever the answer was to that question, there was no doubt that the West tried to copy what made Japan successful at that time by emulating the TPS. They called it by many names like World Class Manufacturing and Continuous Flow Manufacturing, but it was still the Lean methodology at its core.

Lean's popularity soared even further amongst manufacturers in 1988 when somebody named John Krafick wrote the article "Triumph of the Lean Production System". It was just supposed to be a thesis for his Master's Degree at MIT Sloan but it eventually became the basis for further research and a by-word for manufacturing companies.

As a testament to its high applicability, Lean today is not only limited for manufacturing ventures. It can be used for other fields like Education, Construction, Information Technology, Software Development, and other industries.

Benefits

The Lean system does offer a number of advantages to you if you apply it on your projects properly. These include:

A. **Better Customer Service** – The lean method puts a great emphasis on delivering value. By giving exactly what the customer needs, then the manufacturer should be able to provide for a better customer experience.

B. **Improved Productivity** – Productivity in the Lean method is all about improving the output of the manufacturing process. However, it also involves increasing the value provided by each product while also eliminating factors that reduce its overall efficiency in the production process.

C. **Quality** – The Lean method is particular about setting up quality checks. This should reduce defects in the products as well as the need to have them reworked.

D. **Innovation** – Through a series of brainstorming sessions and implementation of creative ideas, the product is enhanced by a considerable degree.

E. **Waste Reduction** – The lean method addresses several key production issues such as inefficient use of space, production of unnecessary physical waste, and optimizing the logistics of key resources.

F. **Better Lead Times** – The team should be able to respond to changes in the project's requirements and reduce delays.

G. **Better Inventory Management** – In the lean method, the team should reduce the amounts of Works in Progresses (WIPs) in its inventory. This should prevent bottlenecking which can further lead to delays.

Why Obsess with Waste?

As you might have noticed by now, the Lean method is rather focused on eliminating waste. But why the strong obsession with it? The reason for this is that Waste can take on many forms. For manufacturing projects, they manifest through unnecessary motion, copious amounts of unneeded byproducts and refuse, and unused materials.

Waste is easy to observe in projects where the processes and end product are tangible (or easily observable). But what about projects whose processes are not seen because they are all relegated in a computer? What kind of waste can you imagine from something like, say, developing software?

The truth is that Lean acknowledges all kinds of waste, not just physical ones. Lean would describe waste as anything that the customer would not pay for and would definitely not agree to be created through the project. To put it in other words, waste is something that exists because of a production but does not add any sort of value to the end product.

The Lean project management calls waste as "Muda" which is Japanese for "trash" or "useless". By identifying the Mudas in your project development process, you can optimize on your team's every moment that is related to producing something for that project.

What are the Mudas of Lean?

It's true that Lean is designed to address various production-related problems for every project. In fact, how Lean works for you is going to be different from other project managers.

But if you do want to know how Lean could be effective to your project, it is best that we go back to the source of it: Toyota. What prompted the company to develop Lean in the first place? During the 1970s, Toyota faced a number of challenges when they were streamlining their production line. The Lean method calls these challenges as "Areas of Waste"

A. **Transport** – A production line may move things that are not necessary for that phase of the process.

B. **Inventory** – How does the facility organize its materials? Can a person there tell components apart from finished products? How about the storage of raw materials and waste products?

C. **Motion** – Every motion that a production facility makes must be optimized. Any procedure that generates a lot of motion without contributing a lot to the development process should be eliminated. This includes unnecessary steps in the process or redundant procedures.

D. **Waiting** – Usually a problem with collaborative efforts, waiting is simply the act of one team having to wait for another to complete their part of the process before they can begin theirs. This also includes delays in the delivery of materials necessary to start or continue the production cycle. Long waiting times are considered waste as they leave several parts of the production process inactive.

E. **Overproduction** – Oftentimes, production facilities create more than what is needed. Their quality notwithstanding, an overproduced batch can take up unnecessary space in the inventory.

F. **Over processing** – This occurs when you devote more resources to a part of the development process than what the standards have required.

G. **Defects** – This is perhaps the most telling that your production system has flaws. It can be caused by a lack of quality inspection or assurance, substandard materials, or outdated processes in the production cycle.

H. **Underutilized Skills** – Exclusive to the Six Sigma method, this type of waste is primarily associated with the knowledge and skills pool that you have set up for that project. It can be arising from your team's skills being inadequate for the task or that you as a manager are not tapping into their full potential for the entire project. This usually happens when you hire people that are overqualified for the job or place them in positions where they cannot fully display their abilities.

What are the Types of Lean Project Management?

Perhaps unlike its other project management siblings, the Lean methodology can be further broken down into 3 sub-types.

1. Kanban

Without giving much away of the process (since it will have a separate chapter dedicated to it), here's the quick rundown of this methodology:

Kanban is a process that is named after the Japanese word for "card". This means that Kanban is a more visual variant of the Lean system as it puts heavy emphasis on making the team communicate more clearly either verbally or non-verbally. The end goal, of course, is to make sure that everybody is on the same page.

Another major feature in Kanban is that it categorizes task queues so as to reduce wastage in the development process while increasing the product's value. Tasks here can be categorized under "Doing", "To Do", and "Done" or other similar terms. Of course, Kanban is a system that can be optimized using Kanban-ready software.

2. Lean Six Sigma

The more statistics-heavy approach to Lean, Lean Six Sigma is designed to remove 3.4 defect Parts Per Million (PPM) in the production process. Lean Six Sigma does this by identifying root causes inherent in project management with a strong focus on eliminating waste in time and resources.

Lean Six Sigma is broken down into 5 phases, which gives rise to its alternative name, **DMEDI.**

- **Define** – Here the goals and the scope of the project are identified along with the value needed by the client.

- **Measure** – How is success achieved in the project? What does it look like? Here, the team sets and quantifies the metrics of which success can be achieved for the project.

- **Explore** – Can things be done more efficiently or is the current production layout adequate? The team should identify different strategies for achieving key points of the project here.

- **Develop** – The team must then come up with a highly applicable yet fool-proof project plan. This can be done by assessing the requirements of the project and the overall budget for it.

- **Implement** – The team then starts the project while adhering to the specifications laid out in the project plan.

Six Sigma is a methodology that works best if you use certain tools. If you do opt to use this version of the Lean Methodology, you best equip your team with the following skills and strategies.

A. **Value Stream Mapping** – What does the project look like in various phases of the production cycle? This has to be visualized by the entire team so they know what to do for each phase.

B. **Research** – The team must be able to rely on outside sources such as customer feedback and focus groups in resolving recurring issues in their development process.

C. **Root Cause Analysis** – It is easy to point to something as the major factor in the occurrence of a problem. But is it really? Root Cause Analysis helps the team understand the underlying issues that plague their development process as well as its symptoms.

D. **Charts** – Visual media like Gantt Charts, Bar Charts, and Statistical Progress Control Charts help the team in understanding how they are faring in a particular phase of the process.

3. The Deming Cycle

This method is based on the Kaizen tools of lean project management and popularized by W. Edwards. The methodology is defined by four phases abbreviated as PDCA.

A. **Plan** – The problem must be identified and analyzed.

B. **Do** – Solutions must be developed and designed to address that problem.

C. **Check** – Upon implementing the solution, the team must then monitor their progress. If improvements are necessary, the team must make them as soon as possible.

D. **Act** – The team will then execute the plans as revised.

The Deming Cycle is actually useful when taking on recurring projects.

For instance, you could start by organizing an impact analysis during the Planning phase. Then, you could follow on this by assessing what worked and didn't in the previous processes while also determining if things were bottlenecking there.

Then, in the Do phase, your team would be attempting to identify solutions to certain problems.

In the Check phase, you can monitor the quality of the solutions as well as their effectiveness in addressing the problem.

Finally, in the Act phase, you could make some improvements on the solution. On paper, this allows you to improve on the quality of the project whenever the production cycle begins anew.

Apart from the manufacturing process, the Deming Cycle is also useful in Software development with its iterative nature as well as construction. In fact, this method is highly applicable in projects with a tiered or systematic production cycle.

Implementation

In order to implement the lean management process, you have to know first the Toyota principles. Use them as a point of reference or inspiration as they form the cornerstone of this agile philosophy.

To summarize, here are the principles.

1. Develop plans based on long-term thinking (as opposed to short term financial goals)

The people that form part of your team should have a sense of purpose to achieve their goals. A good motivation creates a clear vision wherein your team can align themselves to the goals that were set up for the project.

As such, it is your job to identify gaps or waste in the project management and development process. The team's ability to learn from the mistakes of past iterations will ultimately determine the success of the current one and in all projects to come.

After all, there are more worthwhile pursuits in a project than a Return of Investment and short-term profit.

2. Highlight Problem Areas by Creating a Continuous Process Flow

Your team should not focus on improving the project one task at a time. You should focus on improving the entire project management process as a whole

This principle must never be forgotten if your team comprises more than 10 persons. A constant need to innovate the process will also be necessary in improving the development cycle.

3. Use "Pull" Systems to Remove Overproduction

How would your team know when to stop producing or shipping products to a client? For starters, the client would tell you to stop. However, there are also other cues that you can use to stop overproducing and overprocessing.

You should keep the communications between the client, the team, the shareholders, and the management as direct and transparent as possible. You can also use software like Trello to sync your work with the needs of the client and the set production schedule.

4. Divide the Workload Evenly

Do remember that each of your member has a defined role to play in the project. If they feel overburdened or can't catch a break due to the schedule, the quality of their work dips.

As a project manager, you should prioritize quality over quantity. Make sure each team member has enough of a time to focus on part of the project at a time. Assign tasks on each person based on the overall workload that they can handle per development cycle.

5. Create a Culture of Fixing Problems

All members of the development team should have a say on implementing solutions. In turn, they should not feel afraid to voice out their concerns or even alert everybody else on a potential quality issue.

This also means that you and your team should be open to feedback either from within the group or outside.

6. Maintain Consistency of Tasks for Continuous Improvement and Employee Engagement

Project managers must create a standardized process through maintaining quality control checklists and making sure that everybody follows standard operating procedures. Without standards or parameters wherein success can be achieved, your team can't do its job properly and the project's quality won't be improved.

7. Focus on Reliable and Tested Technology to Improve Project Management

As was identified a few paragraphs ago, your team's success under the Kanban variant of the lean management process depends on you using the recommended tools and strategies.

8. Empower Leaders and the Team

Your team must have a constant drive to innovate and this won't be possible unless you set up a command structure where people see leaders and senior members as mentors, not just people to take orders from.

In addition, the team members should be exposed to the latest training and tools that could help them carry their work more efficiently. When people feel that they can grow and improve under the team, the team will become more innovative which helps in keeping the lean method sustainable.

9. Make a Decision Based on Consensus

There are times when projects do not meet the client's expectations. However, you can avoid this from happening by following these parameters:

- You Have to Know What is Going On

- Determine the Root Cause of Each Problem that Surfaced

- Consider all the Alternatives presented to the Team

- Create a Consensus on the Resolution

- Communicate the decision using tools and strategies that are efficient

10. Create a Learning-Based Organization through Constant Reflection and Improvement

The last thing that you would want for your team to become is Stagnant. The environment on which the team works on should be conducive enough for constant learning and personal development.

132

This also means that your team must take the time to discuss what has been done so far in each segment of the project. This would provide everybody the opportunity to find out where they are doing great and where they're lacking. Consequently, this helps them create solutions that address the former.

The point is that your team should not possess the same quality of skills and tools after the completion of every development cycle. Instead, it should be better and more efficient with each project that it completes. The more a team grows and evolves, the better suited it is in completing projects on time.

Lean and Agile

In the field of software development, there is a strong tendency to confuse Lean with the Agile methodology. The truth is that they are actually separate philosophies. Lean is its own thing and is in no way a variant of Agile like Scrum or XP.

But here's the thing, though: they share many similarities which is why you can't fault people for thinking the two are related. In fact, they share almost the same set of qualities which include:

- Adopting a culture where the employee does not burden all the blame which increases buy-in in the Lean method and efficiency in the Agile methods.

- The need for a strong facilitator, not a manager, to ensure that the project stays on track with the schedule everybody has agreed to following.

- Eliminating actions that are wasteful or redundant, replacing them with ones that are efficient and straightforward.

- The act of streamlining processes to ensure that promises are delivered on time.

So what makes them different from one another? For starters, lean is more extensive than agile. It focuses on making the process as efficient and waste-free as possible while also delivering benefits that would be felt across several more projects in the future. Agile, on the other hand, is simply a method to ensure that whatever the customer has envisioned for the project will be translated to something tangible in every iteration.

In addition, lean is best applied across large numbers of people, through multiple groups, or with a large organization. Its overall goal is to encourage efficiency among people while also improving the performance of different related systems. Agile, alternatively, focuses on streamlining the decision making process for specific projects and teams. It is not meant to be applied for works and elements outside of a particular endeavor.

Chapter IX: Kanban

The premise of Kanban is rather simple: by limiting what your team has to do, the group becomes more productive. And when you think about just how much time is lost because everybody is aiming to do so many things at once, you will see why Kanban's premise is attractive.

Kanban is not as widely accepted during the early years of the Agile Software Development movement. This has something to do with the fact that it is a relatively newer (or technically speaking, more recently known) work management methodology. But there is a chance that Kanban might just be the better alternative if you feel that Scrum is restrictive in its design.

How did Kanban Came to Be?

Although Kanban as a methodology has only been recently accepted, the kanban (note the emphasis on the lower case k) concept itself has been around since the mid-20th century. Kanban is a Japanese term that translates to "visuals" or "card".

Like the Lean method, Kanban was developed by Toyota during the 1940s and was partly inspired by Japanese grocery stores. The reason for this is that Japanese stores, unlike their western counterparts, do not overstock. Instead, they store only what is needed or in demand by people and would signal their suppliers only if they need more.

Thus, Toyota came up with this system of using kanban in their production facilities. These visual aids would signal the rest of the production line that some parts are needed or to stop supplying them with materials for now.

Kanban eventually formed part of a movement in Japan called Just in Time. Under this philosophy, Japanese companies only produced and shipped what was needed. By not making more than what's needed, these companies were able to conserve a lot of their resources. And if you consider what Japan had to go through for the mid-1900s, such a system was greatly effective.

Waste and Eliminating It

Upon hearing the word waste, you would immediately think of all those unwanted byproducts in your manufacturing or development process. In essence, waste for you is the things that you produced that nobody would pay for.

But waste in the Kanban method is actually more comprehensive a concept. To explain this, here's a scenario:

Supposed that you run a car manufacturing facility and one of your teams is assigned with making and installing tires. Would it make sense for them to create 1000 tires while a client just ordered 5 cars? No, it doesn't.

Or how about if you are a software engineer and you have an entire group dedicated to adding features to a software. Do they start their work even if the designing team has yet to come up with a concept? No, they don't.

But it would make sense for either team to start working on what they were assigned at the moment that they are given the signal. So, for the car facility, perhaps someone in the production line puts up a Kanban signaling the tire people to start producing tires.

Or, for the software team, somebody puts up a signal saying that the concept has been verified and that the main developers have started building on the primary code. The point is that you can avoid a lot of waste in your production process if people only worked on what is required on that moment for that specific phase of the project.

Of course, you don't have to learn intricate hand signals or put up actual visual aids in your production line in order to implement Kanban properly. Instead, signals are emanated from looking at the overall Work in Progress at any given moment.

So, in a Kanban management program, you might want to signal your feature builder team that the main code is ready. You might put the task on a column that says "Code Ready". This gives the signal to everybody else that you are about to pull a new task and place them on the workload.

By focusing on what is important for that moment, Kanban should help in minimizing waste in your entire production process.

The WIP Limit

Unlike other methodologies that use timeboxes and deadlines to dictate what needs to be done, like in Scrum, Kanban uses something that is called as Work in Progress (WIP) Limit.

WIP limits are, as the name implies, constraints on the amount of items that an individual, a team, or an entire organization is actively working on.

The general rule in setting WIP limits is that they should be slightly constraining. A good starting point is the number of team members working on the project plus the number 1.

Say, there are 10 team members who are working on a specific e-commerce website development project, and the tasks that can be completed for the entire undertaking number in the hundreds, albeit with some tasks requiring only a few hours and others requiring weeks and massive effort. At any given time, the entire team should be working on only 11 tasks. The project manager would just have to make decisions as to which ones are urgent depending on time-sensitivity and the cost of delays.

These tasks are presented in a visual manner through a tool called a board in which tasks are presented in a chart grouped according to status (e.g. Developing, Ready, Testing, Deployed, etc).

If a team goes beyond that limit, waste would be part of the system. And when that happens, that limit becomes a formalized part of the Kanban production process.

The beauty of WIP limits is that they are actually more flexible than schedules, perhaps even more flexible than what Scrum uses. They can vary from one person or team to another and from one phase of the project to another.

So say, a sub team for your project composed of 4 people have a WIP limit of 20 on their Doing column on the Kanban program. This means that each person would be attending to 5 tasks for that phase.

However, the limit of work being reviewed might be different from what was set. This depends greatly on how long this piece of the project needs to be finished and how many people are being allocated to it.

As such, you as the project manager should constantly monitor the WIP limit for each team in each part of the project to ensure that work is done according to the specified quantity. Nobody exceeds and nobody falls short.

What are the Pillars of Kanban?

The WIP Limit might be the heart of Kanban but the methodology still relies on some core principles. In order to successfully implement Kanban, you have to adhere to the following:

1. Visualize the Workflow

Kanban is primarily a visualization method as it helps you see the flow of work with your team. And a key tool here is the Kanban Board where the entire process can be presented in a highly visual form.

However, you should not be so deadest in following the board as the metrics for success can change mid-process. The visualization is only there to remind you and your team what to do now and what to prepare for next.

2. Limit the WIP

The WIP is simply the number of items that your team should work on at any given time. A limit must be set here so that your team does not exhaust itself in one phase, leaving no energy for the other parts of the process.

There are a number of benefits to be had from limiting your WIPs per person which are the following:

- Work Gets done Faster

- Feedback is Acquired Faster

- You deliver more value to the customer in every step of the process

- You minimize the switching of context

- You can anticipate bottlenecks and prevent them from happening

- You don't leave too much work unfinished in the next parts of the project

So what is the ideal WIP Limit then? There is actually no set formula as each team or person has their own limit depending on their skills. Just make sure that every person in the team is doing enough tasks in the project.

3. Measure the Flow and Manage

A Kanban team must always put the WIP first and foremost. To do that, they have to focus on three artefacts:

A. The Kanban Board as it helps them see what tasks need to be done and to prevent bottlenecking. B.

B. Work metrics like lead time, cycle time, throughputs, and queues which help them analyze the flow of work and resources.

C. Project retrospectives to make necessary improvements in the process and remove critical flaws and constraints.

4. Make Process Policies Explicit

Depending on how you make your Kanban board (more on this later on), you will notice some interesting entries which take the form of "rules" for each stage of the work process.

These rules are made when teams identify places where they need to improve on the process. If a flaw is discovered, then the rule should be like "Avoid doing X so that this Flaw Y can be prevented" or something to that effect.

Rules help in removing the more ambiguous elements of the work process while making sure that everybody understands the conditions that they agreed to follow. The less a worker has to interpret something in the workflow, the fewer mistakes they will make.

5. Use Models to Recognize Improvement Opportunities

This goes without saying but you should always communicate progress to your team. This comes in the form of charts and graphs that help people understand what has been achieved and what remains to be done.

By visual presentations, your team can quickly put two different elements together and understand how the quality of one part of the project will affect the rest. With this, they can implement improvements where necessary without having to be told to do so.

Unlike Scrum, Kanban is not that particular in defining how work must be done or managed. It does not even require you to do regular meetings with the team or set up unique roles that persons have to fill in.

The methodology will assume that you and everybody in the project is operating under a notion of project management but you want to improve on it. In short, you already have a system in place already but you feel that you want to take things a bit further.

This means that Kanban is rather easy to implement as you only need to build on what has worked for your team up to that point. There is no need to redo your entire management process and philosophy from scratch just to do Kanban right.

Kanban is also a methodology that is ready to adapt to sudden shifts in the work environment. No two teams in the Kanban method, even if they belong to the same mother group, will implement the system in the same way.

This should make sense as bottlenecks are different from one team or another. The workload of one team might be heavy for another and what strategy one team thinks is effective in addressing an issue might be ineffective for another.

In essence, the core message of Kanban is this: development teams should think for themselves even if they use the same tools and systems. You and your team are always permitted to use Kanban, modify it to fit your project's specifications, and develop a process that is unique to your group.

With this, Kanban should help your team develop a unique value to your clients, streamline the allocation of resources and skills for each project, and manage the risks that might arise from your production process.

Scrum vs. Kanban

More often than not, Kanban is seen as a direct answer to Scrum. To an extent, you could even see it as an alternative. As such, it is of no surprise that some teams would like to move from Scrum to Kanban.

So what makes Scrum different from Kanban and vice versa? Here are a few points.

A. **Cadence** – Scrum projects are usually divided into segments or "sprints". This means that it is a purely iterative production system with each sprint being a self-contained cycle that still correlates with the others.

Kanban, on the other hand, presents a continuous workflow. There is only one Work in Progress but and the team makes sure that they ultimately deliver the composite parts that make up that end product at the end of each phase.

B. **Release Methodology** – Due to its iterative nature, Scrum makes sure that the team offers something functional and tangible at the end of each iteration. This means that they have to present a working product to the client in every Iteration Review.

In Kanban, the cycles are not so defined but the team still aims to deliver something in set periods. Better yet, they have full discretion as to when and how they are going to deliver value to the client in every phase of the project.

C. **Project Roles** – In Scrum, there is the Product Owner, the Scrum Master, and the Development Team. They all collaborate with each other to ensure that the product is improved in every iteration.

In Kanban, there is no defined roles. In fact, the method assumes that you already have a defined system for the project as it focuses more on delivery under that system as opposed to replacing the structure entirely.

D. **Key Metrics** – A major defining metric in Scrum is Speed. Goals have to be achieved on time or before it and value must be given to clients at the end of every cycle as set.

For Kanban, the metric is Cycle Time. Simply put, everybody must follow the sequence as set during the planning phase, doing work only when it is necessary.

E. **Change Philosophy** – Although welcoming to Change, Scrum still insists on teams doing their job of completing the goal. This means that change is still viewed as something adversarial that the team has to adjust to.

In Kanban, it fully embraces change. Metrics and goals can shift in the middle of the project and it is the team's goal to make sure that their work would completely adjust to the new conditions.

F. **Core Principle** – Scrum is a variant of Agile which makes it ideal for close-knight groups working on individual projects. Kanban, on the other hand, is a derivative of Lean which means that it is to be applied on an organizational basis.

Implementing Kanban

Transitioning into a Kanban system is not actually that hard. As was stated, Kanban is already content with whatever system you are currently employing and build on that.

But it does demand for you to follow a sequence so that your team can embrace its principles. Here's how.

1. Start from Where You Are

It is a common misconception in Kanban that you have to re-do everything from scratch to transition to the method. However, Kanban is not requiring you to adhere to some new artifacts or events.

It only asks that you start with what you have now. What are your existing roles and processes? What is only necessary in Kanban is that you follow set procedures but strive to improve them according to their guidelines while also taking ownership over the development process.

2. Set a Kanban Workshop

Kanban is relatively straightforward but don't be fooled by it. It is actually that demanding and would demand a lot of discipline from your team in order to implement it properly.

This is why a workshop must be held before implementing the system. Here, the team can get acquainted with Kanban's principles and how to make it compatible with the current production processes and philosophies.

3. Coming up with a Kanban Board

Now that you have understood the Kanban principles, it is time to build on your board. To do that, you must first understand what a Kanban Board does for your team.

- The Board follows a three-stage flow of work. In other words, all tasks are to be classified as either To Do, Doing, or Done.

- The board is not a ticketing system. The completion of one task does not open the others. Instead, it simply visualizes how each task is interrelated to one another.

- The To Do column serves as your project backlog. It should be prioritized in order of Importance. In practice, this means that the most pressing of tasks need to be placed higher in the list. The more of a priority an item is, the better its quality should be.

  However, do not spend too much time planning things further in the backlog. This is because priorities can change depending on outside conditions. Plan just in time.

- The Doing List is where top priority items from the To Do list are to be placed when their schedule is up. As these are the things that your team is currently working on, it is best that you limit the WIP Limit at

149

this stage. The lower the limit, the fewer backlogs there will be, eliminating bottlenecks.

- The Done List is where items you have completed will be moved to next. The goal here is to get valuable work flowing through your team as quickly as possible. This means that an item must move from To Do, Doing, and Done in the littlest amount of time possible.

So what does your Kanban Board look like? If you want to keep it simple, the board should be comprised of nothing but three columns: One for To Do, another for Doing, and another for Done. That's it.

The point here is that the board should be straightforward to help your team see what needs to be done next and what has been done for that time period. You could also use digital Kanban Boards provided by Kanban-compliant software. They are easy to build and would adjust their data in real time as tasks are completed.

Just keep in mind that this table is just the first iteration of the board. It will change over time as you explore Kanban more. So, just keep things simple for now.

4. Hold Retrospectives Regularly

Once your Kanban system has been set up, the next challenge to face involves making incremental changes to the process. After all, Kanban is only good if you can commit to improving on your current layout.

This is where a Retrospective comes in but you might be surprised that Kanban's retrospectives are not exactly compatible with the ones that Agile uses. This is because the Agile retrospectives are not exactly fine-tuned towards looking at metrics or even consider experimentation.

So how should you do a Kanban retrospective? There is no definite process, but you could take a look at the following aspects.

A. **Open** – Here, you should do a quick check-in activity to start the process and engage with the team.

B. **Last Improvement** – You should review the last experiment or activity that the team has performed. What did everybody learn here? What should be retained? What should be discarded in the next phase?

C. **Kanban Board and Other Metrics** – Review the workflow done by your team. What does the data show you on what needs to be done? As for the things that have been done, were they performed adequately or on-time?

D. Generate Insights – You have to discuss with your team on what challenges they were facing in that part of the development process. What were the constraints that dragged them the most? Alternatively, what aspects of the process did help the team out the best?

E. Next Improvement – Once key issues are identified, you and your team should agree on an experiment aimed to directly address that problem. Use a hypothesis-based format like this: "We believe that (Improvement) will result in (Outcome) while also addressing (Problem). We know we have succeeded when (Metric) is achieved.

F. Close – To end the retrospective, summarize what has been discussed and reiterate what the team needs to do next.

Alternative Step 4. Replenishing the Kanban Queue

So Kanban is not exactly that particular with review and retrospectives. What's your best replacement for such then? Your team can use something called a Queue Replenishment Meeting. These meetings are designed to refocus the team's efforts in prioritizing the work backlog i.e. the "To Do" portion of the board.

These meetings must happen at regular intervals, but they don't have to be done that often that they take valuable time from your team. Time, mind you, that could have otherwise been spent on making the system work.

For example, if you release new content every week, the queue replenishment meeting can be done once a month. Whatever timing and frequency you choose for these meetings, you have to always make sure that it is consistent.

This is because a steady cadence for queue replenishment meetings reduces costs for calling and holding the meeting while also providing certainty and reliability with the development team's relationship with the rest of the company. As such, and if possible, have some of the people higher up and involved in decision making join with the team in these meetings.

These people more often than not can provide more contextual detail and a perspective that your team might have yet to tap into. But always keep in mind that the goal in these meetings is to produce a Backlog from which the team can work with confidently and to the best of their abilities.

And with this, you are ready to implement Kanban on to your project.

Chapter IX: Making Kanban Work for You

If you do choose to use Kanban as your Agile methodology, you have to remember that the whole premise of the framework is to change little of your existing system; if it could be helped. Also, you should have mapped out how things go from Point A to Point Z before you even think about improving the system.

If you do that right, you should at least make your team and system compatible with Kanban. That is but the first part of the challenge, the next part would actually involve you making the most out of what Kanban has to offer. And here's how:

Always Focus on Quality

First and foremost, your team should commit to providing the highest possible quality in the work. Quality is a rather subjective term, mind you, as what one team considers to be of good quality is different from another. And that is even if both teams are working on the same department.

As a rule of thumb in Kanban, however, quality should always be this: the product or component being produced must be at its best possible form before you move on to the next phase of the project. This means that your development team should minimize the team it spends correcting defects by avoiding in making them in the first place.

This does hold true to the goal of Kanban of doing work when it is only necessary. For example, you don't need to allot tasks to fixing bugs and glitches in your software if you already have an optimized system of quality assurance set for it in previous phases.

The more accurate your team is in conducting its work, the less movement it makes or wastes. This in turn maximizes the time allotted for that part of the project.

Reduce Works in Progress

More often than not, quality is assured if the Work In Progress Limit is lower. As such, this step must be implemented in tandem with the one above.

The reason for this is quite simple: if a particular member of your team has a lower WIP limit, then they have fewer tasks to accomplish. This means that they can devote more of the allotted time in refining the quality of their output in each tasks.

So, in practice, a person with only 3 tasks per segment of the project has a better chance of providing 3 quality outputs.

Conversely, a person tasked with 7 tasks per cycle has a lower chance of producing 7 quality outputs.

Now, what is an adequate WIP limit is different from person to person. There is no hard and fast rule as to how much your team members have to individually tackle for that project. As such, you only have to make sure that the WIP Limit for each person of your team reflects their current skills and capabilities.

Deliver as Often as Possible

Similar to its Agile brethren, Kanban is best if you can constantly deliver something tangible and valuable to clients at the end of each set phase of the product. Yes, you are building just one product for the entire project but, at the very least, your team should show progress at each set segment.

For example, you might show a working Alpha Model of the software a few months after the start, then a more enhanced Beta Model by 4 more months. And, finally, a few months before the due date for mass production, your code should be stable and the features you included are functional.

To put it simply, you and your team should deliver on what you promised (and more) in every period that you have agreed to present something to upper management and shareholders.

So why be consistent in the delivery of features and a working code? Not only is this something expected from professionals but it does build trust between the team, the upper management, and the client.

Also, it helps the client get an impression of what the end product would look like once the development process is complete. Perhaps they want some changes or enhancements to be done which helps the team adjust their work accordingly for the next phases. And this makes for a perfect segue into the next tip which is...

Find a Balance between Demand and Output

More often than not, it is at accepting new tasks that your team is going to find a lot of challenges at in the Kanban process. So how can you still provide quality if there is more work to be done while the deadline has not been pushed for even a day late?

More often than not, you will find yourself having to find a way where quality can still be provided even if the WIP limits of everybody else has to be increased. And, of course, you'd rather not risk encountering a bottleneck in the later stages of the development process.

This is where Slack comes in which are short bursts of extreme activity in your production and development process. Keep the slacks short as possible so you don't overextend your team while they still deal with the new tasks in the To Do list. In short, Slacks are the best way for you to balance the demand with the promised output under the Kanban process.

Prioritize, Prioritize, Prioritize

When there is no unpredictability in your team, prioritization does not matter. But, we all know that even the best planned projects have to deal with a certain degree of unpredictability. Not everything is going to be implemented as planned.

So what can a project manager can do to balance things through the project. The answer is in prioritization and your Kanban board will be your primary source of information here.

When new tasks are added into the To Do list, priorities can change. Suddenly, what was topmost priority a few days ago is irrelevant today. It is your duty as the project head, then, to constantly monitor the influx of new tasks and how their presence in the To Do list would affect the ones at the Doing and Done list.

This is also an effective means of preventing bottlenecking in your tasks. If certain new requests come through, they might render upcoming tasks unnecessary to perform. As such, there is a strong chance that new customer demands might not affect the respective WIP limits of your team or, better yet, reduce it.

Attack Sources of Variability

More often than not, you have to deal with variability in your projects as it is the one that can increase WIP limits tremendously while lengthening development cycles. Of course, variability and unpredictability is unavoidable in projects. It only becomes alarming if you have more instances of variability in your project than normal. This often means that your team has actually lost control over how the project should be done.

To avoid this, you must set a distinction over what elements you can control and cannot in the project. If possible, you should have more controllable aspects of the project than those that are variable or unpredictable. This is a telltale sign that your team is actually adaptive to sudden changes in the project, not an entire slave to it.

And when the team does reach a high level of maturity in the Agile philosophy, you can start experimenting with process policies. Which ones need to change so that you and your team can be more adaptive? Are your process policies now hindering you from maintaining agility in the project management process? You can try out different strategies at this point but just make sure that you still produce the expected quality of content even as you are trying out new things.

Conclusion

Learning of all these different Agile methodologies is all well and good. However, we still have yet to answer the most important question of all:

Which one's right for my project?

To answer that question, it is best that we briefly go through what we have learned over the course of this book.

Scrum

As the most popular agile model out there, this is the best strategy that you should use if you want full control over the incremental changes in your projects. With sprints that can go in between 1 week to 1 month, the short development cycles ensure that your team is frequently delivering on the software and features you have promised to a client.

And aside from control, Scrum is ideal for those that are used to (or want to) decentralizing their internal decision-making process. A shared responsibility and voice under the Scrum procedure allows every developer to take full ownership over the entire project. And if they feel that they have a say on what goes next, your team will most definitely go all out in ensuring that tasks are done on time.

Here's a brief breakdown on what responsibilities that each member of the development team should abide by:

- The product owner creates the vision and handles the business and political aspects of the project.

- The Scrum master directs and facilitates the development process, making sure that each team member brings out the best possible results from their work. They are tasked with the more managerial aspects of the process such as eliminating obstacles, organizing meetings, and monitoring the progress done on each iteration.

- The Development team focuses on the more technical aspects of the project such as the building of the code, adding the features, performing quality assurance, and post-launch support.

If your team consists of no more than 15 people per project and wants to remain independent from outside interferences during the project, then the Scrum methodology is your best option.

Extreme Programming

Out of all the Agile methodologies out there, XP is the one most ideal for any project that involves software development. It has a short iteration of 1 to 3 weeks with a strong focus between the constant collaboration between the developers, the upper management, and the development team.

It adheres to principles such as a simplistic design, seamless and transparent communications, constant feedback, and following a well-defined set of coding standards. As such, XP is ideal for projects that span multiple iterations and are inherently complex in nature like, well, software development. It is also the best option if plan-based methodologies are not working for you.

Lean and Kanban

Although not exactly Agile methodologies themselves, Lean and Kanban are related to Agile in the sense that they also focus on streamlining the development process. Where Agile focuses on keeping things short, Lean focuses on keeping things efficient. In essence, no movement should be wasted and the output should only be made when it is truly necessary.

A major focus on Lean, especially the Kanban variant, is the need to continuously improve and deliver without straining the team. In fact, it follows three basic values, which are:

- Visualizing tasks within the context of other tasks and priorities.

- Minimizing the Work in Progress Limits to produce output of better quality in each task.

- Improving the Workflow currently employed by the team instead of outright replacing it.

This methodology is ideal if your project has no limitation on size or team makeup. Also, this might be the best methodology if the specifications of the project require constant output without a defined deadline.

To put things simply, there is no superior methodology in Agile that is applicable for all types of projects. Each method has its own strengths (and weaknesses) that you should be mindful of in order to bring out the best possible results.

However, do keep in mind that the end goal of Agile is always the same: Make teams deliver on their promises frequently, collaborate with stakeholders and upper management constantly, and do adjustments and changes to the overall project strategy whenever the need for such arises.

And this does give rise to another question:

Will Agile Work for my Project?

The short answer is yes. You have to remember that software development has greatly changed in the past few years. The overall dynamic climate of the industry means that any methodology that is dead-set on its own philosophies and strategies would not prosper under the current conditions.

In fact, the rate of failure has relatively increased in recent years. More projects are getting delayed as the base code of most products have become more complicated to keep stabilized. Things like higher development costs, poor planning, and an ever-expanding scope of competition can also affect the development process which results in inferior products.

As such, you are better off using a methodology that is flexible enough for change but is efficient enough to get things done on time and with minimal changes to the overall cost. And that is something that the Agile methodology is quite good at.

And aside from streamlining the development process, the Agile method is ideal in improving how your team interacts with other persons involved in the project. From the higher ups who make key decisions for the project to the client whose vision the team must translate into a tangible product, there are multiple overlapping relationships that are integral to the success of a project.

The agile methodologies can put equal emphasis on human interactions just as much as it does with tools and processes. Furthermore, it focuses on getting things done despite uncertainties rather than following protocols and other constraining systems.

Ultimately, the Agile method is a framework that is best for people that understands that unpredictability is a naturally occurring that must be met with the proper response while not losing sight of what must be eventually achieved through the process. And if that description fits you and your team to a degree, then going Agile might just be the best possible decision you could ever make.

And that concludes this book. Thank you for reaching it this far. Now, you should have a good grasp of what Agile is and how to implement it on your projects. All that is left to do is to act on your plans and see the results for yourself.

Good Luck!

Thank you

Before you go, I just wanted to say thank you for purchasing my book.

You could have picked from dozens of other books on the same topic but you took a chance and chose this one.

So, a HUGE thanks to you for getting this book and for reading all the way to the end.

Now I wanted to ask you for a small favor. **Could you please consider posting a review on the platform? Reviews are one of the easiest ways to support the work of independent authors.**

This feedback will help me continue to write the type of books that will help you get the results you want. So if you enjoyed it, please let me know!

Just go to:

https://www.amazon.com/review/create-review/

Resources

Books

R.Wysocki-Wiley (2009). Effective Project Management: Traditional, Agile, Extreme.

K. White (2009). Agile Project Management: A Mandate for the 21st Century. Center for Business Practices.

R. Russell-Bernard, B. Taylor (2017). Operations and Supply Chain Management. John Wiley & Sons.

J. Malik (2013). Agile Project Management. Schroff Publishers and Distribution.

M. Layton, D. Morrow (2018). Scrum for Dummies. John Wiley & Sons.

K. Rubin, A. Wesley (2013). Essential Scrum: A Practical Guide to the Most Popular Agile Process.

K. Laudon, J. Laudon (2013). Essentials of Management Information Systems. Pearson.

J. Sutherland (2015). Scrum: The Art of Doing Twice the Work in Half the Time. Rh Business Books.

D. Astels, G. Miller, M. Novak (2002). A Practical Guide to Extreme Programming. Prentice Hall PTR.

J.   Pinto (2007). Project Management: Achieving Competitive Advantage. Pearson/Prentice Hall.

S. Pautsch, C. Hanser (2014). Lean Project Management. Verlag GMBH.

D. Pomfret (2009). Lean Project Management: A Study of Application. Project Management Institute.

S. Cimorelli (2017). Kanban for the Supply Chain: Fundamental Practices for Manufacturing Management: Second Edition. CRC Press.

M. Hammarberg, J. Sunden (2014). Kanban in Action. Manning.

D. Summers (2009). Quality Management: Creating and Sustaining Organizational Effectiveness. Pearson/Prentice Hall.

Videos

Infoworld. (2018, March 19). How the Agile Methodology Really Works. Retrieved from: https://www.youtube.com/watch?v=1iccpf2eN1Q

Mark Shead. (2016, May 31). What is Agile? Retrieved from: https://www.youtube.com/watch?v=Z9QbYZh1YXY

Jim Sterling. (2016, April 18). The Jimquisition: Crunch. Retrieved from: https://www.youtube.com/watch?v=Z8RCVoUWJgE

Kim Justice. (2017, May 8). The Agony and Ecstasy: The Story of Duke Nukem Forever. Retrieved from: https://www.youtube.com/watch?v=dfV4rI_gR1g

Henrik Kniberg. (2012, October 25). Agile Product Ownership in a Nutshell. Retrieved from: https://www.youtube.com/watch?v=502ILHjX9EE

Development that Pays. (2017, January 18). Scrum vs. Kanban: What's the Difference? Retrieved from: https://www.youtube.com/watch?v=rIaz-l1Kf8w

CA Technologies. (2016, June 7). The Difference Between Lean and Agile. Retrieved from: https://www.youtube.com/watch?v=aUd3xTdtXqI